W9-BJC-461

What Health Experts Are Saying

"Data from Social Security records demonstrate that hypertension, with its many complications, is a leading cause of disability and premature death in this country. This book opens a window of hope."

> Herbert Doggette, Deputy Commissioner
> Social Security Administration
> National Headquarters

"This book offers a new and original approach for blood pressure control that deals with the problem on the basis of lifestyle change. I believe it will prove to be most successful."

> Mervyn G. Hardinge, M.D., Ph.D., Dr. P.H.
> Dean Emeritus and Founder
> School of Public Health
> Loma Linda University
> California

"You have succeeded in putting together a very interesting and varied collection of anecdotes, scientific references, and a very practical guideline which, taken together, provide a smorgasbord of fifteen choices, any combination of which should result in lowering the diastolic blood pressure to more acceptable limits. I will bring your book when it is published to the attention of the Committee of the National Heart, Lung and Blood Institute."

> John Karefa-Smart, M.D., M.P.H.
> Former Assistant Director General of the
> World Health Organization
> Chairman of the National Heart, Lung and
> Blood Institute Ad Hoc Committee for
> Minority Affairs

"A very definite positive step in the right direction for most patients whom we encounter with hypertension."

Robert DiBianco, M.D.
Division of Cardiology
Department of Medicine
Georgetown University

"I feel the program is a well-developed, carefully managed one to which I would have no hesitation in referring patients."

Wayman Wendell Cheatham, M.D.
Endocrinologist

"Every person suffering hypertension should have a copy of this book."

May Chung, President
Hawaii Health Foundation
Kailua

The Plus 15 Plan for Health Enhancement

15 DAYS TO
LOWER BLOOD PRESSURE
& CHOLESTEROL

Samuel L. DeShay, M.D.
Bernice A. DeShay, R.N., M.P.H.

First Printing, July 1990
Revised Edition, September 1992

Printed by
Review & Herald Graphics

© 1992, Samuel L. and Bernice A. DeShay
All rights reserved
Printed in the United States of America

Cover design, art direction and photography by
Ed Guthero

Library of Congress Catalog number: 92-61868
DeShay, Samuel L.
  Plus fifteen : 15 days to lower blood pressure and cholesterol / Samuel L. DeShay
  p.   cm.
  ISBN 0-945460-16-3
  1. Hypertension – Popular works. 2. Low-cholesterol diet. I. Title.
  RC685.H8D46   1992
  616.1'3206 – dc20
  92-61868   CIP

Scripture quotations are from the *King James Version* of the Bible.

For More Information, Call:
Plus 15 at (301) 891-6052

Affectionately dedicated to our daughters,
Joy and Teymi

Acknowledgments

We would like to thank the following people for their contributions to this project:

Jocelyn Peterson, clinical dietitian and consultant to Plus Fifteen;

Dr. James Hammond, psychology consultant;

Dr. Jacinth Brooks, researcher;

Grace Thomas, Gwen Brown, Gary Swanson, Denese Ellis, Dr. Ernest J. Steed and the host of others who have encouraged us through the years.

Mylas Martin

Dawn Reynolds

Contents

A Note From the Author

Plus Fifteen is a medically controlled lifestyle approach to the treatment of high blood pressure and cholesterol levels without the use of drugs. It is programmed into a series of steps over a period of fifteen days.

Various estimates indicate that some 60,000,000 persons in the United States alone suffer with hypertension or high blood pressure. More than 90 percent of hypertensives are classified as "essential hypertensives." Two-thirds of these are classified as mild hypertensives. Plus Fifteen is designed largely for the *mild* hypertensive, but has been found to be useful for many of those with higher levels of pressure.

The classification of the type of hypertension is based on the diastolic blood pressure level as follows:

Mild Hypertensive—90 to 104 mm Hg

Moderate Hypertensive—105 to 114 mm Hg

Severe Hypertensive—115 mm Hg and above

Please note that Plus Fifteen cannot guarantee that your blood pressure will restore to normal in fifteen days and in no case are you to stop taking your medications without the advice of your physician. In fact, a doctor's clearance to begin this program is mandatory for your own safety.

Plus Fifteen is designed to assist those patients who are

serious enough about their own health status that they are willing to do something about it.

Before you begin, it will be helpful to familiarize yourself with the following terms:

- **Millimeters of mercury** (mm Hg): Blood pressure is measured in small units which represent the amount of force within the blood vessels. The reading indicates how much liquid mercury the pressure can support.

- **Systolic**: When the heart chamber contracts (squeezes) with each beat, blood is forced into the vessels. This is called "systole" and the blood pressure measurement at that instant is called the "systolic" pressure.

- **Diastolic**: When the heart relaxes after the beat, it is referred to as "diastole," and the lower number is referred to as the "diastolic" pressure. The level of the high blood pressure is usually based on this value.

- **Hypertensive**: A person who consistently maintains blood pressure readings above 140/90 mm Hg.

- **Normotensive**: Anyone whose blood pressure readings remain below 140/90 mm Hg.

- **Essential or primary hypertension**: High blood pressure is referred to as "essential" or "primary" when the cause is not known or detectable.

- **Secondary hypertension**: "Secondary" hypertension refers to that type of high blood pressure in which another ailment altogether has caused the problem. When that problem is removed, the blood pressure may return to normal.

For length of days, and long life, and peace,
shall they add to thee (Proverbs 3:2).

Prologue

"Come in, please!" The interpreter beckoned to an elderly man. Slightly stooped and loosely draped in a grayish woolen blanket, he appeared at the doorway of the examining room. A woman followed close behind, with a facial expression that told of the many life struggles she had experienced. A young man entered with them, his shrunken skin suggesting dehydration and weight loss.

The woman spoke in concerned tones. "We want you to look at my son. A few days ago my other son came home, then developed a cough and died. Now this, my last son, has developed the same sounding cough. Can you care for him?"

One with a trained eye could see from their costume that these were people of the Fulani tribe of northern Nigeria. This tribe is fairer in complexion than the other tribes in Nigeria, and the people frequently have straight hair. Their facial features are sharper than the tribes to the south. Typically, they are devoted to raising cows and are very often nomads, wandering from place to place, taking their cows to graze and eventually to market. When traveling on the highways one often spots a Fulani home beside the road, characteristically a grass hut, suggesting the temporary nature of the structure.

Following a hasty cursory observation of the lad, I asked him a few questions and then proceeded to examine him. My first impression of his illness pointed toward pulmonary tuberculosis. I referred him for admission to the isolation ward of the Jengre Seventh-day Adventist hospital in northern Nigeria. His spasms of coughing worried me, and his spitting up was not encouraging.

Over the next few days he appeared improved. When making the hospital rounds, I found him with a ready smile waiting to greet me.

His mother inquired, "How much money should we pay for his treatment?"

"Ten pounds [approximately $40] should be adequate," I answered.

"We may have to sell one cow to get the amount, Doctor, but we will pay," she replied.

At Jengre, no financial statements are made at month's end, no debit reminders given. If the people owe the hospital they most often will return to pay up their debts, even after receiving their treatment. This woman was willing to sacrifice a valuable cow for the healing of her son's cough. Life often forces us to decide what is really important. To the Fulani woman, her son's health was more valuable than the cow. Decision-making becomes a process of weighing values. How much easier the decision becomes when the value of one action (a son's health) clearly outweighs the value of another (giving up a cow).

Many habit patterns we acquire are not really valuable. In fact, probably a number of our habits we cherish may actually cause harm. It would be well to find a way to part with these unfortunate practices. After all, it is not really a sacrifice to give up something that has little value.

Exchanging useful life for that which in essence has no value makes good sense. When I look at it that way it removes the ill feeling, the heaviness, and drudgery experienced in giving up a habit which I may enjoy but which actually destroys my life. It then becomes a joy to give it up, a lesson in character building.

Few people realize that much of their future health and longevity is actually in their own hands. What you invest determines largely the magnitude of your reward. So also is this true for this experience you are now embarking upon.

The Plus Fifteen program offers you a method to lower blood pressure through a more sensible lifestyle, a zero-cholesterol diet for fifteen days and a safe exercise program. In addition, there are several novel approaches to lowering blood pressure, including thoughtful reflection and meditation on spiritual themes.

The key to the entire program, as with most things that are worthwhile, is your investment of time in the program. You must give the appropriate attention to the steps necessary to gain your results.

Before you embark upon the Plus Fifteen adventure you must check on a few items:

1. Comprehensive Physical Examination

You must make an appointment for a thorough physical examination with your doctor before you begin the program. This will avoid pitfalls that may have serious consequences if overlooked. It will also give you peace of mind that you are physically able to complete this program. Additionally, it will bring your doctor into the picture with you so that he knows what you are doing and why.

2. Clearance to Exercise

Not everyone is fit to enter a relatively demanding exercise program. Only your doctor can clear you for participating in an extensive walking program as is taught in Plus Fifteen. Until he has given you this important clearance, you should not begin this program.

I repeat, *do not begin this program until your doctor has given you clearance,* indicating your fitness to exercise under the Plus Fifteen program. This is critical, since your exercise plan is one of the most important adjuncts in this adventure.

3. Shopping Excursion

Look at your menu items (Appendix A) and determine the items you must purchase for your adventure. Natural foods prepared without added salt, or little added salt, is your goal. It is important that you place a strong emphasis on fresh foods in your diet, with an abundance of fruit. Buying for three days at a time is a useful way to begin.

4. Fifteen-Day Commitment

A commitment letter in duplicate is included in the packet. Please sign both copies and return one to Plus Fifteen as you begin. This allows us to record you in our computer for follow-up after you complete the program, and it also allows you to reflect seriously on the whole program as you think through this important procedure.

5. A Buddy Is Helpful

It always helps to have someone go through the program with you. This allows for support and for camaraderie in the process. When you get to feeling down or discouraged the support of a friend is often all you need to make it.

And now you are ready to begin!

. . . a time to keep silence
and a time to speak (Ecclesiastes 3:7).

1

What They Forgot to Tell Me About High Blood Pressure and Cholesterol

Our family moved to Nigeria in 1961 to work in a small government-owned hospital near Port Harcourt, administered under contract by a Christian mission agency.

One of the most important lessons I learned in the new culture was to adopt a simpler lifestyle and the discipline of "not having." For a while we purchased imported frozen foods and other trappings of our American way of life. But because this was so expensive, we gradually weaned ourselves from this cultural dependency.

After more than twelve years of medical practice in Africa, I realized I had seen only one confirmed heart attack in all the thousands of patients I had treated. It happened one day while we were swimming at the Ife University Club in Nigeria. An Englishman had gotten into the pool to swim and developed chest pain. He began to experience difficulty breathing and his color became blue. He was rushed to the nearest hospital. The indigenous people had never seen a disease like this and were fascinated with his color change. He had suffered a heart attack. Following initiation of his treatment and early rehabilitation, he returned to England.

Twelve years of treating patients in Africa and only one confirmed heart attack among the many thousands of cases seen — and that was a European who happened to be there on a business assignment!

I began to wonder why these Africans didn't suffer from heart disease, high blood pressure and dangerous cholesterol levels like we do. My long-time translator, Jeremiah Ajee, would ride his bicycle twenty miles to work each day and twenty miles home. Walking long distances was commonplace, part of everyone's daily routine. It became apparent to me that lifestyle was an issue here.

A recent article from the *Internal Medicine World Report* caught my attention:

> A fifteen-year study by M. John Murray, M.D., of the University of Minnesota, reported that of almost 23,000 African tribal nomads, he could find "no coronary heart disease that could be established by clinical studies. . . . The major cause of death in this group is increasing debility with old age or infections."[1]

Tribes Without Hypertension in Aging Populations

As people age in the U.S.A., it is common for them to suffer from high blood pressure. Some estimates suggest that for persons above age sixty-five, as many as 50 percent may suffer this phenomenon.[2]

Yet some tribes around the world are apparently doing something right in their lifestyle. Hypertension is virtually absent among them. At least fifteen tribal groups from varied races are free or nearly free of hypertension. It is not universal for blood pressure to rise with age.[3]

When Samburu warriors enter the Kenyan army and urban life, they undergo considerable changes in their dietary habits as well as their physical activity levels. Changes were observed in body build and skin-fold thickness, and eventually the systolic blood pressure began to rise. It is also interesting that among the Zulu of southern Africa, the mean arterial pressures were reported lower than in American blacks, in West Indians, and in West Africans.[4]

As far back as 1929, Donnison drew attention to the rarity of high blood pressure in the Kavirondo district in Kenya. For persons below forty years of age, the average blood pressure level was 125/83 millimeters of mercury (mm Hg). Surprisingly, in the group above sixty years of age the pressure fell progressively to about 106/67 mm Hg. Similar results were reported in eastern Uganda, though the pressure did not fall in the older age group. Studies of isolated Melanesian population groups in New Guinea revealed similar results with diastolic pressures falling with aging.[5] A number of such communities have been identified around the world. All have a low salt intake, are physically active, and lean.[6]

Drug Treatment of Mild Hypertension

Strangely enough, one needs to consider a second powerful argument in the approach to high blood pressure control without drugs. In instituting drug therapy for the moderate and severe hypertensive, there was no question as to its value and its benefits for longevity. However, for patients with diastolic blood pressures of 90-104 mm Hg (the largest percentage of hypertensives), drug therapy has not consistently been proven to be beneficial. For the estimated 40,000,000 persons with mild hypertension, there is no conclusive proof that the benefits of drug therapy outweigh its disadvantages.[7]

Health professionals need to be more sensitive to the problems of treating a patient with drugs when alternative methods would be more appropriate. There is the financial cost to consider and the potential side effects of lifelong drug treatment.

Further doubt has arisen from the publication of the mortality rates among 7,610 Japanese men living in Hawaii over ten years of observation. This study reconfirmed the impact of both systolic and diastolic blood pressure as the most important and independent predictors of total cardiovascular, coronary, and stroke mortality. *Higher mortality rates from cardiovascular diseases, however, were observed among those men who received antihypertensive medication at the beginning of the study as compared with untreated men in every category of blood pressure status, from normal to distinctly high levels.* Whereas this apparently paradoxic finding was said to reflect more advanced severity of the hypertension and other risk factors before the start of the study, the investigators stated that *"after adjustment of age, blood pressure and nine other known risk factors in multivariate logistic analysis, antihypertensive medication remained significant as a risk factor for cardiovascular disease, coronary heart disease, and stroke."*[8]

The decision to begin drug therapy for mild hypertension is not as clear-cut as perhaps we would like it to be. Consider the Veterans Administration study:

The Veterans Administration study dealt with a selected group of men in a particular setting. *In the subgroup of patients with diastolic blood pressures of 90-104 mm Hg, the data did not prove that [drug] treatment was beneficial.* This group, designated as "mild" hypertensives by epidemiologists and other investigators, comprises approximately 60 percent of hypertensive blacks and 70 percent of hypertensive whites in the United States. Thus, *for the largest proportion of individuals with high blood pressure, distinct proof of the benefits of therapy was not really available* when intense national concern for hypertension as a major public health problem was resulting in detection of large numbers of newly designated persons with elevated blood pressures.[9]

This concept was given further support in the book *Internal Medicine*:

Actually, the positive values of stopping all drugs even in fully controlled hypertension is under-appreciated. Even the safest drugs have intrinsic risks. In the Veterans Administration study of severe hypertension, 15 percent of those in whom all drugs were stopped remained normotensive [one with normal blood pressure] for the ensuing eighteen months of observation. It is reasonable to suspect that with moderate or milder hypertension this figure could be much higher.[10]

Repeated Blood Pressure Measurements Before Diagnosis

Another problem exists in treating hypertension. Some patients have been placed on antihypertensive medications after one reading in the danger zone. This has been found to be too hasty. People need to be observed under varied circumstances and conditions to assess adequately the prolonged elevation of blood pressure. Readings should be made on three separate occasions after a ten- to fifteen-minute period of rest and relaxation.

Normal blood pressure varies from moment to moment. Exercise often greatly elevates blood pressure in the normotensive as well as the hypertensive. The pressure must be elevated and sustained at this level before committing one to lifetime treatment.[11]

Other Roadblocks to Treating High Blood Pressure

A physician facing complicated requirements for reimbursement from insurance carriers, high liability expenses in malpractice coverage, and exaggerated costs of medical equipment is under constant pressure to keep his business viable. His or her time is money. This may explain why many physicians find it difficult to devote the time to explore with a patient his health habits and the need for behavior modification.

The companies who provide insurance coverage for the population at large practically ignore the physician's need to understand, advise and teach a patient. To the physicians dealing with these insurance companies, such time is not cost effective.

Charts, diagrams, printed materials and other teaching aids help to alleviate the pressure on the physician by encouraging patients to be partners in the treatment program. But by far, drug therapy is the simplest way out. Other areas of lifestyle change rarely get the attention they require.

The health insurance companies will make a significant contribution to the health of this nation when they are willing to recognize that changing a habit is as important as performing an appendectomy or by-pass surgery on the heart.

How Cholesterol Fits In

Although the major thrust of this book focuses on treating high blood pressure, it's important to realize that the recommendations here will significantly lower your cholesterol levels as well. Lowering cholesterol levels is an added side benefit to controlling blood pressure with lifestyle modification. Changing your lifestyle is the best offensive move you can make in taking charge of your health.

And there was not one feeble person among their tribes (Psalm 105:37).

2

Americans Who Have It and Why

Completed in 1943, the Pentagon was the largest office building in the world at the time. It covers 34 acres and offers some 3,700,000 square feet of usable floor space.[1]

One might say the Pentagon is a reflection of our large-hearted "Texas mentality" as Americans. We like to have the world's largest and tallest buildings. We like to entertain on a grand scale. We like to eat only the best.

Americans are known to be warm and generous people. Yet, there are areas of life where we'd be better off if we were not so generous.

Calories, Sugar, Salt

Some estimates suggest that in India the daily caloric intake is in the range of 1400 calories per capita, and in Africa, 1200-1900 calories. By comparison Americans recommend approximately 2400 calories per day per capita.[2, 3]

Many Americans eat their body weight in sugar annually. The average sugar consumption per person each year is 125 to 130 pounds. Many of today's youth eat sugar as though they had a sugar deficiency, often ignorant of the consequences.[4]

The body requires as little as half a teaspoonful of salt per day. Yet we tend to consume ten or more times that amount. It's part of our generous nature.

Alcohol

America has eighteen million adults with alcohol-related illnesses. According to Health and Human Services facts sheet, our per capita ethyl alcohol consumption was 2.65 gallons in 1984, which represents nearly one ounce per day per person in the United States.[5]

Currently, average consumption of alcohol for all persons older than fourteen is 30 percent higher than fifteen years ago . . . representing a total of 28 gallons of beer, plus 2.5 gallons of distilled spirits and 2.25 gallons of wine.[6]

Nearly five million adolescents, or approximately three out of every ten, have problems with alcohol.[7]

We are a generous people.

We eat *too much*.

We drink *too much*.

We salt *too much*.

History of an Illness

Disease is preceded by an incubation period. For diseases such as measles, this time is a few days. For ailments such as coronary artery disease and hypertension, the incubation period extends over many years or even decades.

One writer suggests that the natural history of untreated disease in an individual has seven stages:

1. Birth
2. Exposure to risks of a particular disease
3. Precursory physiologic changes
4. Early symptoms
5. Frank but not disabling illness
6. Disabling illness
7. Death[8]

If you are aware of the course of events for a particular illness, then you can direct efforts at an early stage rather than await the full-blown picture of the disease to emerge. Many chronic adult diseases originate in childhood.

To determine where one went wrong, one needs to investigate his or her general health habits to grasp a clearer picture of his overall health and lifestyle. To discover the causes of hypertension means reviewing the factors in one's lifestyle that influence personal health.

We know, for example, that in areas having the highest incidence of hypertension, such as northern Japan, people ingest more than 20,000 milligrams (about ten teaspoons) of salt per day. We also know that population groups with low salt intake have virtually no hypertension.[9] In addition, such populations are leaner and more active physically, and eat a sparse diet. Stress on the job is lower and the surroundings are less crowded. There is also an association between alcohol ingestion and hypertension.[10] And for some persons, obesity is an important factor, since the loss of weight frequently is all that is required to restore the pressure to normal.

For many years physicians, by practice if not by philosophy, have approached a patient by identifying existing disease, prescribing subsequent treatment, and preventing its recurrence. Now a concept is developing of a "proneness profile" to anticipate disease rather than identify it after the fact.

According to the World Health Organization, we are experiencing the greatest epidemic mankind has ever faced. In the U.S. alone more than a million people die of degenerative diseases each year, and more than half of all deaths from all causes in this country annually are due to heart and artery disease.[11]

In the first comprehensive statement to the federal government on risk factors in the American diet, Senator George McGovern noted:

> The simple fact is that our diets have changed radically within the last fifty years, with great and often very harmful effects on our health. These dietary changes represent as great a threat to public health as smoking. Too much fat, too much sugar or salt, can be and are linked directly to heart

disease. *In all, six of the ten leading causes of death in the United States have been linked to our diet.*

Last year [1976], every man, woman, and child in the United States, consumed 125 pounds of fat, and 100 pounds of sugar. The consumption of soft drinks has more than doubled since 1960 — displacing milk as the second most consumed beverage. In 1975, we drank on the average of 295 12 oz. cans of soda.[12]

In the early 1900s almost 40 percent of our caloric intake came from fruit, vegetables, and grain products. Today only a little more than 20 pecent of calories come from these sources.[13]

In any attempt to unravel a treatment protocol, one should grasp the importance of the concept of causation, both developmental and pathological, particularly since the incidence is not uniform geographically and specific causative factors have not been definitely assigned. Dr. D. M. Hegsted, professor of nutrition, Harvard School of Public Health, observed that the American diet has become too rich in meat and other sources of saturated fat and cholesterol as well as in sugar. He said this alone may not be so bad if we exercised as we should. But because such a lifestyle is associated with obesity, diabetes, heart disease, and certain forms of cancer, Dr. Hegsted warns, "We cannot afford to temporize. We have an obligation to inform the public of the current state of knowledge and to assist the public in making the correct food choices. To do less is to avoid our responsibility."[14]

The American Heart Association has designated adult high blood pressure, or hypertension, as arterial pressure higher than 140/90 millimeters of mercury. The World Health Organization, however, considers pressure less than 140/90 mm Hg as normal, and pressures greater than 160/96 mm Hg as hypertension. The range between these two standards is considered borderline. *Actuarial data show that men and women whose diastolic pressure exceeds 90 mm Hg have shorter life expectancy.*[15]

In spite of recent downward trends in the occurrence of strokes, coronary heart disease, and non-cardiovascular disease, incidence of high blood pressure is actually on the rise. Dr. James R. Sowers of the Wayne State University School of

Medicine observes that this trend is likely to increase rather strikingly through the next several decades.[16]

The United States Health Survey reported that some 60,000,000 American adults have high blood pressure and that possibly 20,000,000 of these are classified as moderate to severe. This means about 40,000,000 are mild. High blood pressure affects some 15 to 25 percent of all persons surveyed.[17]

In a white suburban population such as used in the Framingham Study, about 20 percent of those surveyed had levels greater than 160/95 mm Hg but almost *half* had pressures greater than 140/90 mm Hg. A higher prevalence exists among the various ethnic groups.[18]

Blacks are particularly prone. Dr. Michael Jacobsen observes:

> For some undetermined reason, hypertension affects blacks twice as often as whites. The death rates due to high blood pressure are more than three times higher in black women under the age of 54 than among white women of the same age. Death rates are more than twice as high in black men under the age of 55 than among white men of the same age.[19]

High blood pressure is divided into two types: primary and secondary. The great majority, 90 to 95 percent of cases, are primary. The cause of this type is yet elusive.[20]

Only about three-fourths of persons with primary high blood pressure know that they have it, and fewer than half of those are on treatment. Of those being treated, only a quarter are under adequate control.[21]

High blood pressure is more common in the aged. Some studies have found that as much as 50 percent of the population over 65 years of age suffer from it. High blood pressure also damages the tissue and vessels of target organs, due to the greater force on their delicate tissues, such as the eye, for example.[22]

Secondary hypertension, on the other hand, is that type of hypertension that often has an identifiable cause and is often curable. This group makes up only about 5 percent of cases.[23]

Secondary hypertension is high blood pressure which is causally associated with other factors. These are not addressed in Plus Fifteen.

For primary high blood pressure, the cure is a lifestyle change in the majority of cases. And the American mentality that more is better may not be better at all.

Health does not depend on chance.
It is a result of obedience to law.[1]

3

The Real Issue

Pastor Harrison had always been very circumspect in his life and manners. Yet his son grew up to reject his father's outlook and he drifted into drugs and alternate sexual life-styles. When the father became aware of his son's practices, the shock was overwhelming to the elderly man.

Within six months Pastor Harrison developed a serious thyroid condition, upper extremity tremors, and a host of other ailments. All of these presumably were partially linked to the severity of his reaction to the knowledge of what his son, whom he dearly loved, was doing.

Mental hospitals and medical-surgical hospitals have been physically separated for many years. Many put little credence in the mental effects upon the initiation of disease. However, a body of knowledge has developed through the years which supports four important concepts:

1. The mind and the body are closely related.

2. Emotions largely affect the body.

3. A host of physical ailments result from mental depression, grief, remorse, guilt and discontent.

4. Disease is sometimes produced by the imagination.

In 1962 Dr. Raymond Adams of the Harvard Medical School reported that a large body of diseases of unknown origin is related to personality factors and stress. Among his list he

27

included such diseases as hypertension, peptic ulcer, colitis, bronchial asthma, atopic dermatitis, hyperthyroidism, arthritis, and headache.

He further points out that three lines of evidence tend to set these "psychosomatic diseases" apart from all others:

1. Strong emotions may alter the function of an organ, causing excitement and derangement, but this function is assuaged by feelings of security and relaxation.

2. Individuals suffering these ailments demonstrate an inordinately high incidence of resentment, hostility, dependence or independence, suppressed emotionality, inability to communicate matters of emotional concern or to differentiate between reality and subjective falsification.

3. When emotional factors are ignored or neglected there is an associated failure in medical therapy.[2]

My father recently suffered a stroke at age eighty-eight, and had to be hospitalized. The news of his condition was related to his eighty-year-old sister. Within twenty-four hours she also had a stroke and required hospitalization. Shocking news has often been associated with the subsequent development of heart attacks, strokes, and other ailments.

The Heart of the Matter

While defining exactly what causes high blood pressure is difficult to do, knowing what high blood pressure is is a matter of studying physiology.

Many years ago when a person developed the venereal disease syphilis, doctors ofttimes told the patient, "You have bad blood." It was a term whose use was unfortunate. Today when people hear the term high blood pressure or hypertension, they sometimes think that their blood is too much, too strong, or too powerful. This is a mistaken concept.

Blood flows uninterrupted through the heart, the arteries, capillaries, and veins. It is constantly driven by the force (or pressure) from the vigorous activity of the heart. If the heart should stop, the pressure would drop to zero immediately.

Thus, blood pressure is largely dependent on the heart and its repeated output of blood, beat by beat.

Blood Vessel Size

Another factor important in this formula is the size and quality of the arteries and arterioles. The *arteries* act as conduits for transporting blood under high pressure to the tissues. The *arterioles* and the smaller *capillaries* are the smallest vessels and act at the level of exchange for nutrients between blood and the tissues. The *venules* collect blood expelled from the capillaries. The *veins* conduct the blood from the tissues back to the heart.

Little resistance is offered to the continuous flow of blood by large arteries such as the aorta. However, when the blood reaches the smaller arteries, the force required to keep the circulation flowing continously is greater. This is largely due to the fact that the smaller diameter of the arterioles demands a greater amount of force to achieve continuous flow through them.

Dr. Arthur G. Guyton put it this way:

> Blood flows with almost no resistance in all the larger vessels of the circulation, but this is not the case in the arterioles and capillaries, where considerable resistance does occur. To cause blood to flow through these small "resistance" vessels, the heart pumps blood into the arteries under high pressure — normally at a systolic pressure of about 120 millimeters of mercury in the pulmonary system.[3]

Blood Viscosity

Blood is a thick, almost syrupy liquid that contains red blood cells (99 percent of the cells), white blood cells (1 percent of the cells) and plasma. Blood cells form approximately 42 percent of the blood volume for a normal man, and about 38 percent for a normal woman.[4]

Among the marvels of the human body, the blood ranks prominently. It transports oxygen and nutrients to all parts of the body. It also eliminates waste. Without blood, life would cease. When one donates blood, a simple check of the percentage of blood cells to plasma (called the hematocrit) is ordinarily done to determine one's ability to be a blood donor. If the percentage is too low, one may be disqualified.

When the percentage of cells in the blood rises, as would be the case in dehydration (inadequate water intake or excessive water loss), there is greater friction or resistance to flow by the blood.

If the viscosity of water is said to be 1, then by comparison, the viscosity of whole blood must be assigned a 3 or 4, since it is that many times more syrupy than water. This means that 3 or 4 times as much pressure is necessary to force whole blood through a blood vessel as compared to the amount of force required to move an equivalent amount of water through the same vessel.[5]

Resistance to flow is greater in the smaller blood vessels, or arterioles. In the vessels whose diameter is below 1.5 millimeters, the cells line up and pass through the vessels in a single line, thus helping to offset the effect of the viscosity.

Viscosity is affected by the speed of flow of the blood. Since the velocity (speed) decreases greatly in these smaller vessels, the viscosity is elevated upwards to tenfold.[6] Viscosity plays its most significant role in these small blood vessels and should not be underestimated in its relationship to blood pressure control.

The Varying Blood Vessel Size

Blood pressure is a function of a pump (the heart), a fluid (the blood), and tubular channels of communication (the blood vessels). These tubular channels of communication are so designed that they exert a powerful influence on the blood pressure level.

Slight changes in [the] diameter of a vessel cause tremendous changes in its ability to conduct blood . . . This is illustrated forcefully by . . . three separate vessels with relative diameters of 1, 2, and 4, but with the same pressure of 100 millimeters of mercury between the two ends of the vessels. Though the diameters of these vessels increase only fourfold, the respective flows are 1, 16, and 256 milliliters per millimeter, which is 256-fold increase in flow. Thus, the conductance of the vessels increases in proportion to the fourth power of the diameter.[7]

To understand the approach taken for reducing blood pressure without drugs, it is most important to realize that methods aimed at relaxing the blood vessels (arteries and arterioles) by physiological means may accomplish the same results as the use of certain pharmaceuticals, but without the inherent side effects.

Therefore the key factor in arterial blood pressure control is the varying blood vessel size feature in the system. If the arterioles are largely narrowed (constricted) with their diameters at their smaller value, then the force required to pump blood through such a system is greater due to increased resistance. On the other hand, when the arterioles are relaxed (dilated), the amount of force required for the heart to pump blood through the system is less.

If the variable diameter of the vessels can be controlled by the application of physiologic methods or means, then a great step has been accomplished in achieving our goal. If the resistance of the arterioles accounts largely for the peripheral resistance, we must carefully reduce this resistance at this level.

> Arterial pressure, both at normal and abnormal levels, is a function of flow and resistance. The mean arterial pressure is the product of cardiac (heart) output and total peripheral resistance (the resistance to flow produced when the arteries are narrowed or constricted). If there is an elevation in either of these latter factors, or in both, higher pressures result.[8]

As we search for a way to lower the type of high blood pressure that occurs in more than 90 percent of the persons with high blood pressure, we must consider the key elements involved in sustaining this pressure:

> Blood pressure, no matter what its level, reflects the relationship between cardiac output and total peripheral resistance. In established essential hypertension, the vascular resistance characteristically is the more significant hemodynamic alteration.[9]

Various antihypertensive drugs reduce blood pressure by lowering vascular resistance:

Alpha-Adrenergic Blockers (Minipress and Minizide): "They result in vasodilation and a decrease in blood pressure."[10]

Vasodilators (Apresoline and Loniten): "Reduce blood pressure by relaxing the muscles in the walls of the arteries, causes the blood vessel to dilate, or enlarge, reducing the resistance to blood flow and, as a result, reducing blood pressure."[11]

Calcium Channel Blockers (Procardia, Isoptin, etc.): "Calcium channel blockers are direct acting vasodilators."[12]

The question under consideration is, then, "Will blood pressure be lowered through the physiological means employed by Plus Fifteen?"

Checking Up On Yourself

The Chinese had an ancient practice in which the physician was compensated only while the patient was well. Sickness became a costly item to the physician who had been paid to maintain or preserve health.[1]

Recent attention has focused on the need for an annual physical checkup. Though some insurance groups have played down the need for an annual physical examination, it has been found that such checkups can substantially reduce mortality from causes such as hypertension and colorectal cancer.[2]

Mortality from seven diseases was 30 percent lower in the study subjects at the Kaiser Permanente Medical Care Program in a sixteen-year study of more than 10,000 members. Half were urged by telephone and letter to come in for annual checkups. The study group subjects were between thirty-five and fifty-four years of age. As a result of the invitations, the study group had 2.5 times as many checkups as the control group, and their mortality rates were 30 percent lower.[3]

There is a difference between a health examination and a disease detection program. Disease detection is an after-the-fact identification, whereas a true health examination should pinpoint possible potential for a health problem prior to its development. It is becoming increasingly evident that what is needed today is a better system which will anticipate rather than identify disease.[4]

Presently, the physician makes a diagnosis only when a

set number or pattern of symptoms and signs prevail. During the extended period while the disease is developing, it is left unlabelled, undiagnosed. One leading researcher has observed that perhaps the time to think in terms of "20 percent of disease X" and "40 percent of disease Y" is upon us.[5]

In the book *Predictive Medicine,* the concept of gradations of disease is explored. The author suggests that smaller variations from normal be explored to the fullest, and that normal does not necessarily mean health. Although 95 percent of Americans suffer dental decay, this does not mean that dental decay is healthy.

We know that in various third world areas cholesterol values cluster in the range of 125 to 150 milligrams per deciliter; yet in America "normal" is considered upwards to greater than 200 mg/dl. This does not mean that normal cholesterol should be that high. Such cholesterol levels promote arterial degeneration. "Normal" suggests the typical, the usual, the average, but obviously not always the healthy. The normal ranges have been adjusted to meet our excesses.[6] Now we can all feel more comfortable, since we are "normal" even though this normal means possible proneness to disease.

Data have demonstrated quite clearly that between 65 and 95 percent of presumably healthy people are not healthy. This conclusion could easily be based on the fact that 95 percent of Americans suffer with some dental disease. A look at the seventeen- to twenty-four-year-olds with one or more chronic conditions reveals a rising trend.[7]

Bob was a popular evangelist who had kept a busy schedule for a long while. He happened to stop by a health fair one day and decided to try it for a lark. They put him through the paces, and he did fairly well until he got to the risk factors for coronary artery disease. When those in charge saw his laboratory results, they warned him to go immediately to his doctor and have something done. He was specifically warned that two weeks would be too much for his heart. Bob felt he was too busy at the present time and decided to take a chance and wait until he had finished his present work schedule. Like many others, he put off that which should have demanded his most urgent attention. Within two weeks he was dead.

All disease is preceded by a period of waiting or of subclinical development (incubation). In some instances the period is very short, such as automobile accidents. In other instances, such as with coronary artery disease, it covers decades before it is detected. In order to be best able to help those who are pre-diabetic or pre-heart attack, we must be able to understand the precise sequence of events and analyze just how they have occurred.[8]

It is important to be able to see health as a large spectrum, with perfect health at one end and the absence of perfect health (death) at the other.

To be alert to the sequence of events that precede the frank presentation of illness is necessary in order to effect any changes or attempts to prevent the ailment from overtaking the individual. Even as far back as Hippocrates, the constellation of symptoms such as obesity, menstrual aberrations, and sterility were recognized as occurring together.[9]

Several of these profiles have developed that have indications important to each of us. The Coronary Risk Profile is an example: smoking, elevated serum cholesterol, hypertension, plus elevated blood sugar.[10]

Is there a cancer proneness profile? For a number of years there has been evidence that a person with a disturbance of carbohydrate metabolism might have a correlation with carcinomatosis. Some studies suggest that there is an association between weight and cancer. There is the suggestion that there is cancer risk between elevated blood glucose levels and increased weight.[11]

Impaired glucose tolerance has been associated with numerous disorders.[12]

Regular checkups are a must.

Personal Health Responsibility

In 1977, the Health Assembly of the World Health Organization decided to launch the movement, "Health for All by the Year 2000." Nearly one billion people are trapped in the vicious cycle that includes poverty, malnutrition, disease, and despair that saps the energy, reduces work capacity, and limits ability to act on the basic requirements for life, liberty, and the pursuit of happiness.[13]

How much can a person do for himself in the area of health responsibility? Is the responsibility for my own health with me or with the state? Is it a shared responsibility? How does religion fit into this picture, if it indeed does fit?

There are many and varied opinions today as to how much responsibility for one's health resides with the individual. I would like to quote a 19th century author:

> Only one lease of life is granted us; and the inquiry with everyone should be, "How can I invest my powers so that they may yield the greatest profit? How can I do most for the glory of God and the benefit of my fellow men?" For life is valuable only as it is used for the attainment of these ends.
>
> Our first duty toward God and our fellow beings is that of self-development. Every faculty with which the Creator has endowed us should be cultivated to the highest degree of perfection, that we may be able to do the greatest amount of good of which we are capable. Hence that time is spent to good account which is used in the establishment and preservation of physical and mental health. We cannot afford to dwarf or cripple any function of body or mind. As surely as we do this, we must suffer the consequences.
>
> Every man has the opportunity, to a great extent, of making himself whatever he chooses to be. The blessings of this life, and also of the immortal state, are within his reach.[14]

Earlier we learned that six of the ten leading causes of death in the United States today have been linked to our diet.[15] Dr. Hegsted of Harvard advised:

> We cannot afford to temporize. We have an obligation to inform the public of the current state of knowledge and to assist the public in making the correct food choices. To do less is to avoid our responsibility.[16]

We have learned that 30 percent of all cancers are directly due to the use of tobacco.[17] The Commissioner of Health in the state of New York stated:

> No other single factor kills so many Americans as cigarette smoking . . . Bullets, germs, and viruses are killers; but for

Americans, cigarettes are more deadly than any of them. No single known lethal agent is as deadly as the cigarette.[18]

The Surgeon General of the United States Public Health Service says: "Cigarette smoking is the greatest preventable cause of illness, disability and premature death in this country."[19]

- Cigarette smoking is the major known cause of cancer deaths (The American Cancer Society).

- Cigarette smoking is a major factor in coronary heart disease (The American Heart Association).

- Cigarette smoking is a serious health hazard (The American Medical Association).

We have also learned that some 35 percent of cancers have been linked to our dietary indiscretions. Heart disease, hypertension, diabetes, and strokes are also linked to our dietary regime. This means that over two-thirds of the diseases that are killing the American people today are the result of doing things that are not necessary and, should we exercise some amount of control, could be avoided.[20]

With the abundance of counsel regarding the effects of smoking, drugs, alcohol, and general intemperance in diet, there is sufficient reason to advise the person who desires a long and healthy life to follow the temperate path.

Cast away from you all your transgressions, whereby ye have transgressed; and make you a new heart and a new spirit: for why will ye die, O house of Israel? For I have no pleasure in the death of him that dieth, saith the Lord God; wherefore turn yourselves, and live ye (Ezekiel 18:31,32, KJV).

Those who have advocated more attention to lifestyle are in the minority, but they have touched on an important factor in disease prevention. The Jewish people were given some 200 laws dealing with the subject of health regulations and principles. The focus of these laws was prevention, not cure. We may have important lessons in this approach that will be instructive to us in dealing with the problems we face today internationally.[21]

In the broad societal attack on disease problems involving all available means to improve health, which we call public health, three main avenues of advance are now open: (1) environmental health measures, (2) health education, and (3) personal health care. . . . Influencing behavior through social action, particularly education, appears to be the most immediately promising channel of attack.[22]

How much responsibility for one's premature death and loss to society, the home, the job, can be passed on to the community? Is the individual free to live to himself and treat his life in such a way that he becomes a burden upon the society in which he resides? When the society is responsible to help support the cost of illness, is it fairness for one to live in a known reckless manner?

In looking at personal health responsibility, I find that little attention has been given to this important phase of the transaction between one's personal responsibility and that of the society to which he belongs. There are important trade-offs that need to be explored in this area.

Are you ready to make some important decisions regarding your health? We've discussed the how's and why's, but unless you take action all the facts and figures in the world don't mean a thing. I encourage you now to commit to the Plus Fifteen adventure that follows.

The doctor of the future will give no medicine, but will interest his patients in the care of the human frame, in diet, and in the cause and prevention of disease.[1]

5

How Shall I Treat It? Let Me Count the Ways

There was a man with an infirmity of thirty-eight years' duration who waited by the pool of Bethesda. It was commonly believed there was periodic healing through the water. The New Testament records that the Master asked him a simple question — which on the surface seemed to be rather obvious: "Wilt thou be made whole?" (John 5:6).

No Treatment

It has always fascinated me that this question should be asked of this man. Yet, it is altogether conceivable that some who are sick do not desire to get well. Some may want to be well, but the effort to do so is too great. Many want to be well only if it is convenient and brought to them at minimal cost. Healing is preferred only if it is instantaneous and effortless.

Many people think nothing of purchasing an automobile for a hefty sum, and they will routinely pay large amounts for regular servicing of the machine. Yet, should you ask them to pay $10,000 to $20,000 for preventive health, they feel the price is too great, the expenditure too demanding.

Dr. Anthony Campolo, the delightful sociologist/preacher

from Eastern College in Pennsylvania, tells the story of a yuppie who had an accident, resulting in a severe injury to his arm. When he came to, he was moaning, "My Rolex, my Rolex," unmindful of the damage to his arm and hand. It would appear that things are more important than people these days.

When we first introduced the Plus Fifteen program, we observed that some sufferers with high blood pressure, though regularly purchasing drug medication at substantial monthly cost, surprisingly would hesitate to enter such a program. I found myself asking the question of them, "Wilt thou be made whole?"

Some do not want to be well if it means any effort on their part. Others are unsure of their own ability to maintain sufficiently a healthful lifestyle over time.

Some persons I have known, when told they have a particular diagnosis such as diabetes, deny that they have it. They look for excuses, for alternative explanations which allow them to continue living in well-established habit patterns. Denial is a common approach for a serious or uncomfortable diagnosis. Those with high blood pressure are not free from this outlook or approach.

My wife used to be the charge nurse of the diabetes training program at a California university in Los Angeles. She became so adept at watching the attitudes and practices of certain diabetics that she could generally pick them out in a crowd.

Typically, they might be found at a lunch counter, grossly overweight, wearing thick glasses, hovering over a hot fudge sundae and savoring every bite. The desire to satisfy an overwhelming and untamed appetite superseded the desire to be well.

"Wilt thou be made whole?" To deny or ignore the presence of a disease as devastating as high blood pressure is to be like the proverbial ostrich placing one's head in the sand to ignore the obvious danger. "No treatment" is frankly stupid.

Drug Treatment

When drugs first began to be used for treatment it was

demonstrated that those with severe (malignant) hypertension had extended survival as compared with those in whom no treatment was instituted.[2,3] Formerly it had been nearly zero survival for the severe hypertensive after one year, rising to 70 to 80 percent survival at one year and nearly 60 percent at five years when medicated.[4,5]

Following this success it was revealed that keeping the blood pressure down also reduced some of the complications. Morbid events were three times higher in the placebo (sugar pill) group as compared with the medicated (treated) group.[6]

The Veterans Administration study also demonstrated that severe hypertensives (diastolic pressure 115 mm Hg and above) receiving the placebo (sugar pill) were in jeopardy when compared to the treated group. The same trend was demonstrated in the moderate hypertensive (diastolic pressure 105 to 114 mm Hg) group. The observation period was terminated with this group based upon the comparison with the placebo-treated group and the implications for life extension in the medicated group.[7,8]

It should be further added that we are comparing drug treatment with no treatment (placebo). It is important to understand this significant qualification of this comparison.

Lifestyle Treatment

Looking at the broad scope of one's approach to health and to longevity, an emphasis on lifestyle pays off in great dividends. There is a powerful example of the effect of lifestyle on the most significant factor we know — longevity! I include it here for your reflection.

Dr. Lester Breslow, dean of the School of Public Health at the University of California at Los Angeles, recently asserted that it is possible, with existing knowledge, to increase American life expectancy by eleven years. His assertion was based upon seven basic health principles or laws commonly known to almost anyone who understands health basics.

I. Avoid Tobacco

II. Limit the Use of Alcohol

III. Eat a Good Breakfast Daily

IV. Avoid Eating Between Meals

V. Get Adequate Rest

VI. Engage in Regular Exercise

VII. Remain Close to One's Ideal Weight

When researchers did studies on these rules and found that they really do correlate with life expectancy, they were convinced. For nine years they studied a group of men and women, comparing lifestyles with mortality rates. At the end of the nine-year period, men who regularly observed all seven rules had a death rate of only 5.2 percent. Those who followed six of the rules—only one less—had over twice the mortality rate. Men who observed three or fewer had a 20 percent chance of dying within the nine-year period, a four-fold increase in mortality.[9]

I would affirm the importance of following the laws of health, which have been established for the human body since the beginning of time for our well-being and happiness.

It has been fairly well proven that reducing the pressure of the moderately severe hypertensive also reduces the susceptibility to some of the major complications. Reducing the blood pressure in the hypertensive by whatever means is a way of prolonging useful life in addition to reducing the incidence of stroke, congestive heart failure, and kidney failure.

The wise Hebrew king, Solomon, observed that "the curse causeless shall not come" (Proverbs 26:2). Postum, the cereal beverage frequently used as a substitute for coffee, carried the slogan, "There's a reason." Disease does not occur without a reason. Somewhere something went wrong. It is important to know what kind of disease a person has. It is equally important to know what kind of person has the disease. Sorting out causation is a complex problem. One must think of what steps led to the development of the problem and how these steps may be retraced and corrected.

In a typical physician's office, it would be difficult to find adequate time to address the many factors in the many patients' lifestyle which have laid the groundwork for the development of high blood pressure. In the preface to his book,

None of These Diseases, Dr. S. I. McMillen makes the following statement:

> This book was born as a result of a thousand sighs for the many people who left my office without receiving adequate help. There wasn't time to do much more than prescribe some pills for their complaints, but I knew there was something better than pills for them to take for the rest of their lives. In this book, I have written the prescription I would have given to those patients if only I had had the time.[10]

Health behavior change is a complex subject at best. The problem involving one's strength of desire for change must be considered. A plan of therapy must be appropriately outlined with time intervals for review. The ability to make a decision regarding treatment is a key factor in the realization of a disease.

At one overseas conference setting I was present when an attendee complained of abdominal pain, fever, loss of appetite, and a change in bowel habit. A group of physicians made a cursory evaluation of his case and ascertained this was possibly an acute appendicitis. Thinking we would get good service for our patient at the nearby hospital, we rushed him to the emergency room only to be confronted with long delays. When the intern finally arrived, he listened to the history and the evaluation along with our recommendations. He then proceeded to interpret the signs and symptoms according to his own perception of the case. He decided not to act, but to wait. He said his superior would be available later that day.

With dispatch, my colleague said, "Let's get our patient out of here before he dies." We took him to a fairly distant reputable hospital where the doctor operated immediately and found a badly ruptured appendix. Fortunately, the patient recovered fully. It was very clear to us that the ability to make a decision is vital, urgent, and necessary.

When one has clear-cut signs of an acute life-threatening emergency and fails to recognize the urgency of his problem, he has made a serious, maybe fatal, mistake. Decision-making is a priority. Decisions on health interventions frequently are delayed because of fear or whether pain is experienced, rather than the severity of the problem.

Yet, by demonstrating interest in your health you can have input into your future. You may help your physician by informing him of your attitudes and desires involving lifelong hypertensive therapy. Tell him to explain the alternatives and weigh the choices for your particular case. He will help you make correct decisions.

Remember, the majority of diseases that people suffer are unfortunately due to either ignorance of, or disregard for, their own physical laws. At least six of the ten leading causes of death in the United States today have been linked to our diet.[11]

Thirty percent of all cancers are directly due to the use of tobacco. This represents some 100,000 lives yearly affected by an unnecessary evil among us.[12]

We have also learned that more than 80 percent of cancers are thought to be attributable to potentially controllable environmental factors. Heart disease, hypertension, diabetes, and strokes are also linked to dietary indiscretion. This means that over three quarters of the diseases that are killing the American people today are the result of things we are doing to ourselves.

When a disease has an environmental cause, the individual has a responsibility for making the change or changes to eliminate or control the disease. You can do it if you try!

Combination Treatment

Those who are unable for one reason or another to get off their medication completely may find that they are able to reduce the amount of medication they are presently taking by incorporating new lifestyle factors into their daily rituals.

Such practices should become a regular part of the daily routine in order for them to be useful and helpful. Often when the medication cannot seem to do the job, the addition of some measure of lifestyle modification may be just the thing needed to push one over the hump into the normal range for blood pressure control.

Who knows? It may just be what you need at this time, if you cannot eliminate your medications due to the level of your blood pressure and the complications that have set in.

Understandest thou what thou readest?
And he said, How can I, except
some man should guide me? (Acts 8:30,31)

6

Can I Do It At Home?

More than thirteen years have passed since my family and I left California to take up a post in metropolitan Washington, D.C. The excitement of returning to the eastern United States was heightened by the thrill and challenge of a new job, new friends, and a new frame of reference.

Not long after arriving in the Washington area, my wife and I realized that the pace of life, the close proximity of urban living, and the potential loss of control in reference to our small children were more than we had bargained for in this move.

Soon we began looking for a spot in the country where we might find peace and solace. (That is a story in itself.) We finally decided on a location that seemed to adequately fit our needs. But we did not have the necessary resources to build a home suitable for our long-term demands. We searched everywhere for help.

One program we came upon was "U-Build." This concept was particularly appealing to us because of our shortage of necessary capital to do the construction at the level we desired. We were surprised at the available help and self-instruction which one could tap for building a house.

America is richly blessed with numerous self-help methods. Bookstores are nearly flooded with instructions, booklets and magazines for the person willing to put forth the effort. There is a certain fascination with being able to say, "I did it myself."

There are four keys to the Plus Fifteen program, which are not part of the program itself, but without which the program will fail. If you're asking yourself, "Can I do this?" the answer is yes, provided you seriously dedicate yourself in these four areas: time, organization, consistency, and commitment.

Time

I once worked as a medical officer in a group of prisons. During my interaction with the incarcerated citizens, I found there was a yearning in the heart for that moment of freedom. Some went so far as to mark off the calendar and religiously record the remaining days to freedom.

People often use the expression, "Time flies!" An inmate awaiting release may not see it so. What we usually imply in this expression is that we have not achieved the results we had expected within the time we were given. What people really mean when they say they don't have time is that the issue before them does not possess sufficient importance to warrant taking time for it.

In a New Testament parable, Jesus spoke of a certain man who prepared a great supper and invited many guests. At supper time a servant was sent to call those who were invited and to tell them all was ready.

The excuses offered for declining to attend were varied. One man said he had bought a piece of ground. Another responded that he had bought five yoke of oxen. A third answered that he had married and therefore could not come.

Interestingly, the excuses given were very weak. The story says the servant was sent to call the guests at supper time. You would not go to see a piece of ground at supper time because it would do no good to see it at night, and though I hold no claim to being a farmer, I am familiar enough with country living to know you don't go to prove oxen at supper time.

Indirectly these excuses let the host know that his invitation was not important enough to these people to necessitate altering existing plans to fulfill the engagement sponsored by the host.

Today many demands press in on us. We have work schedules and leisure activities. Any other intervening programs may be considered peripheral or unnecessary unless the time be exceedingly brief.

Yet, what is more important on this earth than life and the factors to ensure my continued effectiveness as long as humanly possible?

When assessing and assigning your priorities, where does the investment of time point in matters of health and longevity?

To whom do we owe our existence? Is life to be whittled away in frivolity and careless efforts unmindful of aims, purposes, and direction?

Plus Fifteen requires a time commitment, but it's worth the effort. Key to the prioritizing of your time is your belief in the worth of the program for you. Before deciding to go it alone at home, ask yourself if you have the time to invest in your high blood pressure treatment sufficient to complete the program.

Organization

Organization is management of one's self and one's approach to life and leisure. A characteristic of 1200 centenarians studied by Osborn Segerberg included "order." This pattern of orderliness was discernible in the lives of more than 96 percent of the subjects who lived to 100 years.[1]

Life requires planning and organization, and this order is underscored with another important concept—discipline. Discipline is required to set priorities and categorize activity. The end result will be a more meaningful life, complete with its greatest benefits.

Plus Fifteen requires order and organization of one's self to accomplish the necessary items in the body of the program. If you plan to do the program at home, it is important to give consideration to this point.

I am including a suggested daily schedule as a possible

outline for the day's priorities to those people willing to invest the time.

Daily Schedule

6:00 A.M. Rising Time
Take blood pressure and pulse
(this is your baseline reading)
Water Break

6:30 A.M. Spiritual Reflection
Exercise Time (Walking)

7:00 A.M. Hydrotherapeutic Procedure with morning cleansing
Breakfast

10:00 A.M. Rest/Relaxation Break on the job (15 minutes)
Water Break

12:30 P.M. **Lunch Time**
A stroll after lunch outdoors
Sunlight, if possible (20 minutes)

3:00 P.M. Water Break
Rest/Relaxation Break on the job (15 minutes)

6:00 P.M. **Supper** (small)
Exercise Time (Walking)
Happy Time/Spiritual Reflections

10:00 P.M. Retire

Consistency

When I began studying piano at age twelve, my friends were full of discouraging words, "You'll soon give it up," or "You, play the piano? Nah."

Since practice is what makes a pianist, one must decide to discipline one's self to practice. The incomparable pianist Paderewski was said to have practiced eight to twelve hours a day. Some musical measures need to be rehearsed a hundred times until they are firmly in the mind and the fingers. Paderewski developed this personal approach.

Entering a program such as Plus Fifteen requires a dedication to be consistent with the regimen as outlined. Failure to do so is failure of the program.

A warranted argument many researchers bring against lifestyle programs for modification of behavior is that the new behavior is not lasting. They cite examples from weight reduction program participants whose weight loss is often anything but permanent. I have met people who say they have lost 1000 pounds — by losing, regaining, losing, regaining, etc. What a way to go!

We must stress that the consistency with a lifestyle modification program must be equal to the dedication to take a pill.

Practice. Practice. Practice. Why? Practice works. Practice can become habitual. Practice makes perfect.

Commitment

There is nothing to replace this valuable attribute so closely aligned with consistency. Commitment means making a decision to stick with the program.

Be honest with yourself. Cheating on your diet, your salt intake, or on your exercise only hurts you in the end.

Determine that you will wholeheartedly give yourself over to getting control of yourself and your future. Such a commitment will pay handsome dividends in the end.

Block out other desired but interfering activities during your fifteen days devoted to this program. Tell yourself you will not allow intervening issues to cloud or destroy your good intentions.

Remember, giving commitment to the laws of health will bring with it other benefits. "For length of days, and long life and peace, shall they add to thee" (Proverbs 3:2).

Let God take over your commitments, providing you with the strength to accomplish your goal. It can be done. Millions have done it.

The Importance of a Support Network

Plus Fifteen as a program is ideally carried out in a group setting, including instructors, social interaction, and nightly sessions with an opportunity for exchanging ideas and coping methods others have found useful.

There is a certain synergism in doing things with others

faced with similar backgrounds and challenges. This cannot be underestimated in thinking about the subject of this chapter, "Can I Do it At Home?"

Because there are so many areas of living touched in this program, social supports play a key role. When pleasurable experiences must be modified, it frequently requires considerable effort and mental determination to accomplish it. Having people around you who support you during the initial time of instituting lifestyle restrictions is of utmost importance.

On the basis of this factor, you might consider joining a center where such a program is routinely done. Perhaps talking a few friends into doing the program together may be all that is required for you to achieve the necessary social support to accomplish the fifteen steps required for this important and satisfying lifestyle alteration.

When one has been accustomed to a particular way of thinking and doing, alterations and alternatives do not come easily.

How to Get Started

Having underscored the above points, let us look at the question of doing the program at home.

First: *It is mandatory that you see a physician for this program to fulfill four specific requirements.*

1. Approval to Enter a Lifestyle Program

The blood pressure level of certain patients may be such that it would not be wise to attempt to alter the treatment protocol due to the delicate nature of the blood pressure control or the height of the blood pressure. These persons should enter this program only on the advice of their personal physician.

It is not the purpose of the Plus Fifteen to intervene in the relationship between a patient and his personal physician. Rather, we are here as a back-up, offering a plan and program to assist in the control of one of America's most important public health problems, hypertension.

Following Plus Fifteen and its stated outline will not only

help your blood pressure, but will (when carefully followed) reduce your risk for other important diseases, and ultimately affect the length of your life.

Changing lifestyles makes a lot of sense. We believe in it and continue to push that others may realize this as a key to long life and happiness.

2. The Comprehensive Physical Examination

Before embarking on a program which may change your approach to your daily routine, it is necessary to be evaluated to ensure that you will not do yourself any harm by entering a program requiring substantial amounts of physical activity. This is particularly true should you suffer from arthritis, joint deformities or injuries, as well as other potential defects, such as heart disease, previous stroke, or spinal, ankle, or hip malformations or distortions. Such changes require approval from your physician before joining this program.

Those who suffer from heart failure, or have heart pacemakers, a history of previous heart attack, abnormal heart rhythms, diseased heart valves or structural changes in the heart need the approval of a cardiologist before entering this program.

3. Approval to Exercise

Only your doctor can set the limits of your exercise tolerance. He should guide you in your ability to perform the necessary requirements of Plus Fifteen. He will give you a realistic picture of your capabilities and your limitations for physical exertion.

Before embarking on efforts at jogging, or even extensive walking or calisthenics, it is necessary to get a physical examination and a heart evaluation.

4. Withdrawal of Medication

Do not stop taking any medications except on the advice of your personal physician. It is not the place of Plus Fifteen to tell you to stop taking your medication.

Usually by the end of the first week, one may have a

sensation of some lightheadedness associated with a decrease in blood pressure. This often indicates that you are carefully following the program and your blood pressure may be dropping. Your doctor may then want to elect to space out your medications to every other day or decrease the dosage you have been taking.

The key that tells your doctor the program is having an effect is a comparison of your blood pressure readings. You must compare your initial readings with those readings experienced after one week on the program. The gradual descent is a clue to your reduced need for the amount of medication you are presently taking.

Be careful to drink adequate water during the program to insure that your body fluids are adequately maintained throughout this period of adjustment.

It is very important that you monitor your blood pressure daily, taking a reading several times throughout the day all during the Plus Fifteen program. This is your best clue as to how well you are accomplishing your goal. Give particular attention to the basal blood pressure reading which you take after waking up each morning.

Can I Do It at Home?

Yes, you can. If you agree to work under your doctor's supervision and have a clear understanding of what's involved in the four areas (time, organization, consistency and commitment), you will be successful.

It is preferred, however, that you enter a program conducted by knowledgeable professionals, and monitored by a physician.

If the prophet had bid thee do some great thing, wouldest thou not have done it? (2 Kings 5:13)

7

The Plus Fifteen Adventure

There are several legitimate ways to begin this fifteen-step program. Think about which method fits your personality.

1. Check in at a center where this type of program is conducted by staff trained in helping you achieve your goals. This can be on an outpatient or live-in basis.

2. Get the video cassette (available from Plus Fifteen) to simplify the instruction for the steps and watch it as you do the steps at home.

3. Try all the steps for the first fifteen days to orient yourself to the extent of the program and its total impact upon your health. See how differently you feel during this introductory period.

4. If you are a mild hypertensive, you may not require all fifteen steps to accomplish your goal of blood pressure restoration. Salt restriction and appropriate exercise may be all you need. As you see how much change you can accomplish with each step, you may want to focus on those steps with which you are most comfortable as a start. Pick and choose until you accomplish your goal of normal blood pressure: 140/90 mm Hg.

Do not be overwhelmed by the extent of the total program. Rome was not built in a day. The ideal is to be able to practice all fifteen steps regularly as your daily routine. Should this prove impossible, then do what you can, little by little, until you achieve your goal and are satisfied with yourself.

NOTE: Prior to beginning this program, it is required that you have a complete physical examination in order to ensure your capability to perform under the stated conditions of the program. In instances in which heart problems are revealed, a review by a cardiologist is also required.

And now, let's begin!

Step I represents your activity for Day 1 and is simply learning to take your own blood pressure.

Step II is an explanation of the role of mineral components in your diet: sodium, calcium and potassium. On Day 2 you'll also take your blood pressure several times for practice.

Step III is your exercise plan and should be done on a daily basis as described. Also take your blood pressure several times during the day and eat according to the principles in Step II.

Step IV begins your relaxation practice. In addition to taking your blood pressure, following the guidelines for sodium and potassium intake, and exercising the advised amount, add fifteen to twenty minutes of relaxation exercises twice daily.

Step V incorporates into your daily routine drinking water to flush and cleanse your kidneys and using water in the form of arm baths, hot and cold showers and other therapeutic methods. If Step V is done during your regular morning or evening preparations, it does not greatly alter your routine.

Step VI discusses the relationship of nicotine and caffeine to hypertension. If you're a smoker, it's time to quit. There are many programs available to assist you in stopping smoking. The important thing is to *do it*. Continuing to practice the previous steps will help conquer the nicotine habit. If you're a caffeine addict, it's time to kick the habit. Drinking 64 ounces of water each day may help conquer the desire for coffee or cola.

Step VII offers a lighter look at one's self and encourages more interest in the bright side of life. Continue to

• take your blood pressure (Step I)

- eat according to plan (Step II)

- exercise (Step III)

- relax twice daily (Step IV)

- do your water rituals (Step V)

- refrain from cigarettes, coffee and cola (Step VI)

Step VIII is an explanation in more detail about your diet and how to make it work for you.

Step IX demonstrates the effect of alcohol on blood pressure and should be carefully read.

Step X discusses the role of fats. Continue your regular routine mentioned above, adding olive oil to your regimen.

Step XI brings in the concept of light (preferably sunlight or a sun lamp). The use of a sunscreen such as PABA 29 offers protection from damaging ultraviolet light.

Step XII explains the issues surrounding weight control. The prescribed diet should offer considerable help to those struggling with a weight problem. Combine the diet with the exercise plan and you're off to a great start.

Steps XIII and XIV involve long-term effects of environment, work and leisure.

Step XV encourages you to think about where you are headed. Everyone needs quiet time to consider directions, goals, aims, and spiritual implications in life.

There are nine areas which involve *daily* practice and require approximately three hours a day:

1. Taking your blood pressure (10 minutes).
2. Staying on your diet (10 minutes).
3. Exercising as much as is feasible (30 minutes).
4. Using relaxation techniques (30 minutes).
5. Utilizing water as therapy (30 minutes).
6. Taking a lighter look at life (10 minutes).
7. Adding olive oil to your routine (10 minutes).
8. Making use of sunlight (15 minutes).

9. Spending time in spiritual reflection (15 minutes).

Compare this time with the amount you may spend in non-rewarding pursuits or simply watching television. Are you worth saving? You be the judge. How is your attitude toward your value as a person? How much would you feel you can give to improve your health and longevity?

Take some time to answer those questions. Then get ready, get set, let's begin!

The Well-Informed Patient: A Partner

Goals

- Learn how to take your own blood pressure.

Equipment

- Stethoscope (a listening apparatus)
- Sphygmomanometer (a blood pressure monitor)
- A pressure gauge
- An inflatable cuff
- A rubber bulb
- A screw valve
- Personal log card
- Pen

Science Deals With the Measurable

Twenty percent of patients listed as hypertensive from physician's office readings were found by twenty-four hour ambulatory blood pressure monitoring to be normotensive.

—Internal Medicine News

Discussion and Rationale

"Clearly, many people who are being called hypertensive and are being treated don't have it," says Dr. Norman Kaplan, professor of Internal Medicine at the University of Texas, Southwestern Medical School, Dallas.[1]

In a recent study of some 292 patients whose blood pressure readings were in the hypertensive category on repeated office visits, 20 percent were found by twenty-four ambulatory monitorings of their blood pressure readings to have normal levels.[2]

According to this study, fifty-eight people would be committed to a lifetime of blood pressure medication who did not really have high blood pressure but were suffering from what has been termed "white coat hypertension." This simply means that the emotional stimulation of a visit to the doctor was enough to elevate the blood pressure, but this elevation was only temporary and not sustained. For blood pressure to be labelled "high," it must be high and sustained that way over time. Therefore, it is important for every patient labelled "hypertensive" to know how to take his own blood pressure at home. By multiple home measurements during varied activities, a clearer picture will emerge as to the effect of various circumstances on blood pressure readings, providing feedback on one's progress.

It has been estimated that when blood pressure treatment is based on a single set of readings, the blood pressure is likely to be over-estimated in as many as one-third of persons presently on medication.[3]

The popular newspaper *USA Today* carried the headline, "Blood Pressure Too High? Test it again—millions may be misdiagnosed." In their report they suggested that 15 to 20 percent of patients don't need vigorous treatment.[4]

Dr. Richard Grimm, a hypertension expert, says white coat hypertension may well be related to other risks such as stroke or heart failure.[5] Dr. Brent W. Egan called the white coat hypertension "pseudo hypertension."

White coat hypertension is not a form of hypertension but a measuring error and should be suspected when the blood pressure is elevated without any damage to the usual organs affected by hypertension – the heart, the kidneys, the eye and the brain. Another sign might be finding the blood pressure dropping too low when given blood pressure medications.[6]

About 20 percent of patients have their highest readings in the physician's office. The stress of visiting their physician for some patients may parallel the stress which raised their blood pressure in the workplace.[7]

I had an interesting experience with a patient whose blood pressure readings were related to her encounters with her boss, a hard-driving Type A personality who could not accept any less-than-perfect work from his subordinates. When off duty, her blood pressures were fine, but in the highly stressed environment of the office, consistently high readings occurred. When given a period away from the office the blood pressure normalized, but on return to the office setting her pressures again were abnormally high.

The rationale for learning to take your own blood pressure at home rests on the platform of keeping a close touch on what is really happening to your body. Be well informed. Repeated measurements will help attain an accurate assessment of your blood pressure problem.

A great array of prescribed medicines may even overshoot your blood pressure control, particularly at night when the blood pressure falls to its lower values. Researchers are now discovering that the added burden of medication may in effect drop the pressure too low and precipitate other complications.[8]

Consider the approach of the conservative British who outlined their program in the April issue of the *British Medical Journal:*

I. Treat patients less than eighty years old with diastolic pressures over 100 mm Hg only after repeated blood pressure measurements for three to four months.

II. Observe patients with diastolic blood pressure levels of 95 to 99 mm Hg for three to six months. Treat them for high blood pressure only if they are at high risk from their high blood pressure due to elevated cholesterol, diabetes, smoking, complications, or a family history of high blood pressure.

III. Measure the blood pressure yearly in those with initial readings of 90 to 95 mm Hg.[9]

Dr. Norman Kaplan observed that should the United States use these guidelines, we would cut out treatment for about half of the people now being treated for hypertension. He further observed at the annual meeting of the American Society of Hypertension, that "physicians have gone too far, too fast" in treating borderline hypertensive patients.[10]

Taking your own blood pressure, day-by-day, makes a lot of sense. Keeping tabs on your body will help your body to serve you longer.

Method

1. Get into a comfortable position, usually seated and undisturbed.

2. Relax for several minutes before you begin taking your blood pressure reading.

3. Take out the blood pressure monitoring equipment from your package.

4. Identify the parts of the equipment and compare with any accompanying pictures and diagrams.

5. Assemble the parts of the blood pressure monitor as instructed.

6. Follow the instructions for a trial run of taking your own blood pressure.

   a. Locate the pulsation in the bend of your arm (at the level of the elbow). This is the brachial artery. Place your finger on it to identify it.

   b. Apply the deflated cuff snugly around your upper arm, keeping it about one inch above the elbow.

   c. Take the rubber bulb in your hand, making sure it is attached to the inflatable arm cuff, and turn the screw-valve until it closes. The cuff should now be deflated.

   d. Place the stethoscope ear pieces comfortably in your ears and the round listening piece over the brachial artery.

e. Squeeze the rubber bulb enough times to cause the pressure gauge to register a numerical reading approximately 30 points higher than the pulsation at the brachial artery (in other words, when you can no longer feel a pulse at the bend of the elbow, pump the rubber bulb 30 points higher and stop pumping).

f. Immediately turn your screw-valve in the opposite direction in order to open it and allow air to escape very gradually, carefully noting the numbers on the gauge until it fully deflates. The numbers on the gauge should fall at a rate of two to five millimeters of mercury per second.

g. The first thumping sound in a series of sounds you hear is your systolic pressure reading. Continue listening until the sounds disappear completely. The last sound you hear is your diastolic pressure reading. The normal blood pressure value is 140/90 or below.

7. Practice this procedure many times daily until you are comfortable performing it, following carefully the instructions given with your blood pressure equipment.

8. Record your blood pressure reading on a *personal log card* each day (see example below), preferably taken at about the same time, such as on retiring or arising.

Personal Log Card							
	Su	M	T	W	Th	F	Sa
Pulse							
Blood Pressure							
Exercise Time							
Relaxation Therapy							
Hydrotherapy							
Weight							

Sodium, Potassium and Other Minerals

Goals

- Limit sodium to 2000 milligrams daily (some mild hypertensives may have up to 3000 mg daily.)
- Increase potassium intake to 4000 mg daily

Equipment

- Food Tables for sodium, potassium, calcium, magnesium, etc.

Science Deals With the Measurable

A moderate dietary reduction from ten to five grams of salt per day should drop blood pressure approximately ten millimeters of mercury systolic and five millimeters of mercury diastolic.

—F. Gilbert McMahon, M.D.

Mazzola reported supplementing the diet with 1000 milligrams of potassium daily over a period of only two weeks can lower the blood pressure eleven millimeters of mercury systolic and two millimeters of mercury diastolic.

—*Excerpta Medica*

Discussion and Rationale

Sodium

Pauline loved salt on almost everything, even on things most people would not want to salt. She put salt on grapefruit and watermelon, and just about anything else she could find to eat. She had become a salt addict. One day, Pauline collapsed at work. She had to be rushed to the hospital emergency room where her blood pressure was found to be extremely high, 230/130 mm Hg. Her doctor, agitated over her casual approach to her disease, severely limited her use of salt to control her now prominent symptoms.

"There is now overwhelming evidence that sodium [salt] plays a critical role in the etiology [cause] of essential [primary] hypertension, which accounts for 95 percent or more of hypertension," stated Dr. Mordecai Blaustein, professor of physiology, University of Maryland.[1]

Americans generally get about 15 percent of their sodium from the salt shaker. Another 10 percent is that which occurs naturally in food. Estimates suggest that nearly 75 percent of sodium intake comes from processed foods.[2]

Recently on a plane, the flight attendant offered me a drink to pass the time. I requested tomato juice, wanting to do my body a favor and avoid the usual colas and coffee. Graciously, she left me the entire tin. To my great surprise I read that the tin contained over 1000 milligrams of sodium. Shocked and upset, I wondered why the innocent tomato should have that much added salt.

Little do we realize as we leave our supermarket or restaurant that we have purchased a megadose of salt in some of the most unlikely places, thanks to certain food manufacturers.

The typical American may daily consume anywhere from 10,000 (five teaspoonsful) to 20,000 (ten teaspoonsful) milligrams of salt, while 1000 milligrams (one-half teaspoonful) are adequate to meet the body's needs.[3]

Suppose you're from Honshu in northern Japan. The average daily intake of sodium there is among the highest known in the world, exceeding 20,000 milligrams (ten teaspoons) of salt per day. The incidence of strokes (169 percent higher than the U.S.A.) and hypertension (roughly sixty of every one hundred Japanese) is higher than nearly all other places in the world. By contrast, in the Aita people of the Solomon Islands, in which daily sodium intake is in the 500 milligram range, high blood pressure is rare to non-existent.[4]

The National Academy of Sciences recommends that people who do not have high blood pressure limit their salt intake to 3300 milligrams of sodium daily. This is about 1 1/2 teaspoons of salt each day.[5]

Research studies have shown that among normal individuals who brought their sodium intake down to 1600 milligrams from 3500 milligrams daily, blood pressures also dropped. Some scientists feel there are indications that limiting salt as a regular habit for those without hypertension may even *prevent* its occurrence.[6]

According to Dr. Gilbert McMahon in *Management of Essential Hypertension,* "Salt restriction is beneficial to all patients with essential hypertension." He further added that data suggest that a moderate dietary reduction from 10,000 milligrams to 5000 milligrams of salt per day should drop blood pressure approximately 10 mm Hg systolic and 5 mm Hg diastolic.[7]

The dosages of drugs used to control hypertension may be reduced by salt restriction. British researchers Beard and Cooke demonstrated that the doses of drugs used to control high blood pressure could be reduced by fifty percent when salt restriction was added. One third of the patients in their study were able to stop their medication completely.[8]

Potassium

The relationship of potassium intake to high blood pressure regulation has been studied for more than fifty years. It has been shown from numerous studies that potassium has a protective effect in the regulation of blood pressure.[9]

The average American consumes from 2300 to 2800 milligrams of potassium a day. Blacks, who generally experience a more severe type of hypertension, consume only about 1600 to 2000 milligrams of potassium daily. According to one study, there is significant speculation that this very factor may importantly contribute to the higher rate of hypertension in blacks.[10]

Those persons on a high sodium/low potassium diet tend to have more sodium and less potassium in the urine, and also maintain higher blood pressures by significant amounts. When the mean total body potassium content is measured in untreated hypertensives, 42 percent had total body potassium values less than 85 percent of expected values.[11]

Mazzola has reported that supplementing the diet with 1000 milligrams of potassium daily over a period of only two weeks can lower the blood pressure 11 mm Hg systolic and 2 mm Hg diastolic pressure. This amount of potassium can be found in half a cantaloupe.[12]

In northern Japan, Sasaki documented that two villages with similar intakes of salt had differing blood pressure levels. The village with the lower blood pressure was characterized by the fact that they ate an abundance of apples. Apples are rich in potassium.[13]

People on a relatively high salt intake, more than usually advised for hypertensives, were found to have reduced pressures when the potassium in the diet was increased.

Such implications are far reaching and the possibilities should encourage us to consider supplementing the diet with potassium-rich fruits, vegetables and legumes.

Four thousand milligrams of potassium daily is a desired goal, according to researchers at the University of Mississippi.[14] We recommend that amount for Plus Fifteen participants who have normal kidney function. This counsel is also supported by Dr. Keith Ferdinand, cardiologist, Xavier University, who advises blacks particularly to increase the potassium intake to more than 80 mEg (approximately 6000 milligrams of potassium) per day.[15] One author speculates that our ancestors on unrefined diets largely of fruits, vegetables, grains, and nuts typically consumed a diet of approximately 2000 milligrams of sodium and 7000 milligrams of potassium each day. They were largely free of hypertension.[16]

Calcium and Magnesium

Increasing the intake of fruits, vegetables, nuts and grains while decreasing the intake of meat will positively affect the levels of calcium, magnesium, and various trace minerals. This approach is probably safer than giving a blanket encouragement to supplemental calcium or magnesium at this time. Research studies are conflicting as to the value of such supplementation.

Method

1. Set a goal to increase the potassium in your diet to 4000 milligrams daily, if your kidneys function normally.

2. Make a rule for menu items: 150 to 250 milligrams sodium per food item is an acceptable limit. Your total day's allotment for sodium is 2000 milligrams.

3. Use abundant fruit to increase your potassium and to satisfy your desire for sweets. It works!

4. Avoid processed food—the vast majority of salt in your diet comes from these foods. Estimates suggest that upwards to two-thirds of your salt intake may come from these foods.

5. Before purchasing any item of food, check the labels for sodium content per serving. If the information is withheld, do not purchase.

6. Place the day's quantity of sodium in a plastic bag, and use this amount for cooking and seasoning. Do not exceed!

7. Become salt sensitive as you taste food. Emphasize foods that are low in sodium in your diet. Rice is a favorite. It requires little, if any, salt.

8. Take the salt shaker off the table.

9. Get the salty snacks away from the house. They can be very tempting. Replace them with celery sticks, carrot curls, and sliced cucumbers.

Step III

The Exercise Prescription

Goal

- Walk your way to health. It's natural!

Equipment

- Use comfortable walking shoes.
- Dress appropriately for the climate.
- Loose-fitting garments are advised.

Science Deals With the Measurable

Roman conducted a long-term study of exercise on hypertensive females; three months of training three days a week at a moderate intensity (70 percent maximum heart rate) lowered blood pressure by 21 mm Hg systolic and 16 mmHg diastolic. The next three months, his patients practiced no training, and blood pressure rose to pre-study levels. Twelve months of moderate intensity training again substantially lowered blood pressure 20 mm Hg systolic and 18 mm Hg diastolic.

—Cardiology 67:1981

Discussion and Rationale

"I hate these exercise nuts," Tom grunted. "I see them in the streets at morning rush hour. They always make me feel guilty with their sweat suits and constant jogging. My choice of exercise is sitting in my recliner enjoying my TV. Besides, I walk all day at work and I just don't feel like more activity when I get home. I don't think it does any good anyway. Doctors disagree about whether it really will lower my blood pressure."

Up to this point Tom's wife had been silent, but she knew he was fighting that which he most needed — exercise. Finally, she spoke gently to her husband, "Dear, we really want you to live a healthy and full life, and your amount of exercise is not enough. I saw on TV that research has shown that exercise helps lower high blood pressure if practiced consistently."

Tom's wife was right. Numerous studies have shown that high blood pressure can be lowered by exercising on a regular basis. Let's take a look at a few of these studies:

1. One researcher conducted a long-term study of exercise using females who were suffering from hypertension. After three months of training three days a week at a moderate intensity, their systolic blood pressures were lowered by 21 mm Hg and their diastolic pressures by 16 mm Hg. The next three months, these same patients practiced no training and their blood pressures rose to pre-study levels. Twelve months of moderate intensity training again substantially lowered their blood pressures.[1]

2. The American Physical Education Association has repeatedly touted walking as a sane exercise for all people.

> It is a safe, total-muscle-building, heart-supporting, organ-toning, lung-expanding, joint-lubricating, blood-circulating-and-vitalizing, bone strengthening, weight-controlling, disease-preventing, nerve-quieting exercise perhaps unmatched by any other of the aerobics. Dr. Bud Getchell insists that most people should walk, not run, if you want to stick with a fitness program. He notes that the dropout rate for high-intensity exercise like running is more than 75 percent after six months, while more than 75 percent of walkers keep on walking.[2]

3. It has been shown that exercise training can lower diastolic blood pressure at rest and during exercise.[3]

4. In a study of the effects of changing levels of physical activity on cardiovascular risk factors in twelve normal subjects,

> we found that forty minutes' exercise three times a week lowered blood pressure by 10/7 millimeters of mercury below sedentary levels with a small additional fall when exercise was increased to seven times a week.[4]

> Physical training lowers blood pressure in normotensive subjects. . . . A small (2 or 3 millimeters of mercury) blood pressure reduction in the population as a whole may considerably reduce cardiovascular morbidity and mortality. Physical training could be strategy whereby a population-wide blood pressure reduction may be achieved.[5]

> The variability of blood pressure makes it necessary to make many measurements in order to detect a small change after training. The problems of blood pressure variability and the altering response may be avoided if multiple measurements of blood pressure are taken.[6]

> Exercise training might in some patients with moderate essential hypertension be an alternative to pharmacological treatment.[7]

> Pharmacological treatment of mild hypertension has failed to reduce mortality in coronary artery disease (heart attack). Thus, more attention has been focused on non-pharmacological intervention.[8]

5. Dr. William L. Haskell, at a program sponsored by the American College of Cardiology, recently observed that about 80 percent of the cardiovascular benefits of jogging and other forms of vigorous exercise can be obtained with exercises such as brisk walking or walking uphill.[9]

> A regular exercise program can lower blood pressure to normotensive levels over one year.[10]

> We found that exercise three times weekly for one month lowers blood pressure in sedentary normal subjects and in patients with essential hypertension.[11]

Exercise Options

When beginning a program of exercise don't overlook the useful activities and exercise potential of daily chores. Try to think of common activities as beneficial exercise.

Here is a listing of some typical activities with the number of calories burned on an hourly basis for an average man of 176 pounds:

Gardening—250 to 340 calories burned per hour

Shoveling snow—675

Working in the yard—245

Climbing hills—665

Walking, 2 mph—205

Walking, 4 1/2 mph—500

Stair climbing, up—1020

Stair climbing, down—500

Window cleaning—225

Mopping/sweeping—260 to 300

Mowing grass—280 to 300[12]

Exercise as part of daily living is important. If one walks more, climbs stairs instead of taking elevators, then he can reduce his chances of death from hypertension by 28 percent. A report in the New England Journal of Medicine indicated that those who burn 2000 calories a week in such activities enjoy this decreased death rate.[13]

The resting pulse rate (pulse during periods of no activity) is a rough measure of the condition of the heart. When the rate is in the 50- to 60-beats-per-minute range it is more favorable than a 90- to 100-beats-per-minute value.

Light exercise, contrary to typical attitudes, will call for a four-fold increase of blood to the working muscles. Exercise produces heat, causing more blood to be shunted to the skin for cooling. Moreover, strenuous exercise produces a ten-fold increase of blood supply, observed Dr. Mervyn Hardinge in his treatise, *Philosophy of Health*.[14]

A 1980 report from the United States Public Health Service concentrated on exercise. For adults in the eighteen to sixty-four-year-old range, vigorous exercise participation at least three times a week for twenty minutes each session was urged.[15]

For those with knee, ankle or back problems, trampoline exercises may prove beneficial. They can offer the enthusiast a highly efficient form of heart conditioning. Trampolines are approximately seven inches above the floor and have a diameter between three and four feet. One can do running in place, jumping jacks, fast walking, as well as rotating exercises.[16]

We want to urge you to stop taking the elevator and try the stairs. Get up a half hour earlier and spend the time walking. You will feel all the better for it.

Method

1. You must have doctor's approval to engage in this program.
2. Our program involves walking only, with emphasis on exercises for the lower legs.
3. You are aiming at reaching 60 to 75 percent of your maximum heart rate. This is your target. Subtract your age from 220. Then take 75 percent of the resulting figure. This is your target maximum heart rate for exercise.
4. Begin with small increments such as fifteen to thirty minutes twice daily.
5. Gradually increase to one hour twice daily, if feasible, by the second week.
6. Do not overdo it, but be persistent. Stop if you have chest pain, shortness of breath, or irregularities of your heart.
7. Mark off the mileage you intend to exercise using the odometer on your car or a pedometer.

8. Check your pulse before you begin your walk and at ten-minute, twenty-minute, and thirty-minute intervals. Compare these results with your target maximum heart rate.

9. Get a comfortable pace and continue it. Let your common sense guide you on the amount of exercise you can tolerate. Emphasize distance, not speed.

Step IV

Rest, Relaxation and Feedback

Goals

- Get seven to eight hours of restful sleep nightly
- Learn relaxation techniques

Equipment

- Automatic Sensor Card*
- Audio tapes from Plus Fifteen*
- Comfortable easy chair
- Eye shields
- Stop watch

Science Deals With the Measurable

With breathing and group therapy over a twelve-week period, systolic pressure dropped 26 mm Hg, and diastolic pressure 13 mm Hg.

—Internal Medicine News

---

* Equipment items marked by an asterik (*) are included in the Plus Fifteen equipment package. They are highly recommended but not required for the program.

Discussion and Rationale

In his book, *None of These Diseases*, Dr. S. I. McMillen draws a fascinating contrast between a lion and a crocodile. The lazy and sleepy attitude of the crocodile is a familiar one. Generally he lies motionless, just like an old log, hardly blinking an eye. One might say he is a personification of tranquility. He seems not the least bit concerned about keeping up with the Joneses, or even about the bumps and blemishes distorting his less-than-beautiful face.

Dr. McMillen goes on to describe an old lion: eyes dim, gait somewhat unsteady. He even needs dentures at age twenty-five and is just about ready for the happy hunting ground. The crocodile, by contrast, at age twenty-five is hardly changed from his ordinary youthful vigor.[1]

The Cleveland Clinic Museum has stuffed animals from around the world, and at the side of each stuffed animal are exact replicas of the animals' adrenal gland and thyroid gland.

As you probably expected, the lion has a very large adrenal gland. He lived a life filled with stress and his alarm reactions were many. He spent his years in hard fights chasing after less-fierce animals and some not-so-easy-to-conquer beasts. His life was spent in anxiety, hunting, flights, and long night searches. No wonder his adrenal gland and thyroid gland outdid themselves for size.

In the crocodile these glands — the adrenal and thyroid — are remarkably small. His adrenaline demands were fewer. The stimulus for hormones to raise the blood pressure and its resultant destructive effects on the arteries was less.

Some have felt that the number of signals that the emotional center emits largely determines the size of the stress glands such as the adrenal and thyroid.[2]

Notice this: "It has been repeatedly shown in humans that exposures to a more stressful environment will produce increases in blood pressures."[3]

Apparently, lions and crocodiles are not the only animals that have influences on their blood pressure and reactions in their adrenal and thyroid glands. Emotions have a dramatic effect on blood pressure and may largely affect our physiological state as well, a fact not to be taken lightly.

Have you observed the reactions of an audience watching an intense movie or television show? Notice the excitement and involvement of the viewers, and the collective shock when something unexpected happens to a key figure in the story. It has been reported that in nursing homes there is more difficulty getting the patients settled down after a thriller or murder story, resulting in more nursing home violence between patients after watching these types of stories. We often overlook the role of the media in raising our alarm reactions higher and higher.

In a recent publication from the United States Department of Health and Human Services, the following statement is made: "During the past decade, considerable interest has been directed toward the question of whether the effects of stress on blood pressure could be modified psychologically or behaviorally."

The method used to identify this problem was to provide input (feedback) to individuals with high blood pressure on an almost continuous basis using electronic devices. Making use of this information, the patients could develop mental techniques to lower and raise blood pressure based on the immediate feedback from those factors which affected their blood pressure. This method constitutes what is known as the biofeedback treatment of high blood pressure.[4]

It has also been demonstrated that persons with primary (or essential) hypertension show a hyperactive response to stimuli, and this is mediated through the person's nervous system.

Typical responses to daily events and activities make appropriate minute-to-minute changes in blood pressure levels of both those with normal blood pressure readings as well as those with high blood pressure responses. The stressful events around us produce short-term changes. Prolonged stress is a factor in the development of hypertension in groups which have been subjected to especially stressful situations.[5]

It becomes obvious that since stressful situations are

known to elevate blood pressure, relaxation techniques are being sought as a method of treating it. Literally hundreds of papers have been written on the subject of the possible benefits of relaxation and biofeedback techniques on reducing blood pressure.

There is documentation that when humans are provided with feedback for different physiological processes and are reinforced with appropriate incentives for controlling these responses, they can learn to self-regulate functions such as heart rate, blood pressure, blood flow, skin temperature, sweat gland activity, and stomach and intestinal processes.[6]

Plus Fifteen uses the relaxation technique similar to that developed by Dr. Herbert Benson of the Harvard Medical School. It can be done at work, at home, or any place where you can sit quietly for ten to fifteen minutes. Research studies of these and similar mental approaches to tension relief demonstrate that they can relax physical tensions, lower blood pressure, slow pulse rate, and produce a relaxed mental state.[7]

Breathing is also influenced by emotions. Fear, grief, anger and even happier emotions like joy and surprise produce changes in body tension and can restrict breathing. Undue tension will alter normal breathing patterns. We must learn to allow ourselves to breath freely and naturally.

Generally, we make use of less than half our lung capacity in breathing. Fear seems to increase tension, and tension tends to restrict breathing. The relationship of body and mind is often underestimated. What affects one also affects the other.

In an Israeli study reported by Dr. Clara Wittenburg, breathing exercises and group therapy significantly reduced blood pressure in patients diagnosed as having mild hypertension. However, the breathing exercises apparently were the most effective over the long term. The Brelax group which focused on breathing exercises was followed once weekly over a twelve-week period. Systolic pressures dropped 26 mm Hg and diastolic pressures dropped 13 mm Hg during that period. Fifty percent in one group and 58 percent in the other stopped medication entirely for the duration of the study.[8]

Relaxation techniques must be continued on a schedule

similar to medication administration in order to be effective in long-term treatment strategies.

Dr. M. J. Irvine, of the psychiatric research department of the Toronto General Hospital, reported that relaxation and stress control therapy were found more effective than mild physical exercise in controlling hypertension.[9]

According to Dr. Stewart Agnes at Stanford University School of Medicine, the main indication for relaxation training appears to be persons with high blood pressure who respond most poorly to medication. He concludes that relaxation therapy might serve as an alternative to medication for those not responding to an initial trial of regular monitoring.[10]

What does all this mean? Simply put, it means using relaxation techniques regularly has merit in lowering your blood pressure, but only if you practice them consistently.

Method

1. Take a fifteen- to twenty-minute rest break every four hours during your working day.
2. Get 7 to 8 hours of restful sleep each night.
3. Practice the routine of muscle relaxation 1/2 hour daily.
   - Tense 7 seconds/relax 45 seconds
   - Begin with legs (right then left)
   - Proceed up the thighs
   - Then the torso
   - Next the arms
   - Last, the head
4. Try to shut out the world for a while each day and rest.
5. Get some relaxation tapes as soon as possible and make use of them daily. Use eye shades or a darkened room and a comfortable easy chair. Practice listening to the relaxation tapes 1/2 hour daily.
6. It's highly recommended that you schedule biofeedback with an instructor. Try to get in some time each day for this program.

Water
as Therapy

Goals

- Practice one hydrotherapeutic procedure daily.
- Drink 64 ounces of water daily.

Equipment

- Basin for holding hot water
- Water thermometer
- Bath towels
- Ice bag
- Bed/cot
- Shower/bathtub

Science Deals With the Measurable

Prolonged heat to the precordium [over the heart] increases the heart rate, decreases its force, and lowers blood pressure.

— Fred B. Moor, M.D.

Discussion and Rationale

Yellowstone National Park was established in 1872 in northwestern Wyoming, southern Montana, and eastern Idaho. It is the largest and best known national park in the United States. Though it contains several distinguishing features such as fossil forests, volcanic plateaus, and the black osidean mountain (volcanic glass), the biggest attraction at Yellowstone are its 10,000 geysers and hot springs. The best known of these is Old Faithful which erupts to heights of 100 feet every 33 to 93 minutes.[1]

Health seekers have long visited places such as Hot Springs National Park where over 1,000,000 gallons of water flow daily. The average temperature of this water is 143°. The European health spa grew up around the concept of the healing properties of such waters.[2]

In modern times such places do not attract the crowds they once did and the term *spa* has been used to describe almost any exercise room or workout gym around. The benefits of heated water on the body have been eclipsed by a greater emphasis on more artificial means for treating disease and restoring health. The experience of past years, however, bears need of review.

Water — Internally

In their drive to climb Mt. Everest, a group of Swiss climbers became extremely fatigued and weak just short of their goal. They had less than a pint of water per man per day during the last three days of the climb. They failed to make the summit. However, a British party took additional water and found this to be the deciding factor in their successful ascent to the top (five to seven pints per man per day were required).

Dehydration, the lack of adequate water, is a cause of fatigue and weakness, often unsuspected and overlooked. At high altitudes the moisture content of the air is quite low, hence the need for larger amounts of water ingestion. Appropriate operating conditions for our bodies' optimum function require some sixty to eighty ounces daily.[3]

The need for water internally is often overlooked, probably because we depend on thirst as the prompting sign. But drinking even when we're not thirsty is necessary to keep up with the body's demands and needs.

Water — Externally

Heat is easily lost from the body due to environmental changes which in turn affect physiological processes of the body. These changes affect growth, reproduction, the antibody production, and resistance to infection, energy, metabolism, and even mental activity.[4]

When one uses water applications to affect physiological change in the body and to treat disease, it is known as *hydrotherapy*. Generally, the physiologic response parallels the extent of environmental change. Muscles are relaxed under the influence of hydrotherapy as demonstrated by research at Harvard.[5]

Should a person be placed in a bath at 97°, there is little physiologic response. However, should we alter that water to 110°, marked physiological changes occur. These changes include a rise in temperature, and a rise in pulse rate and respiratory rate. The skin also becomes flushed, the blood more alkaline and the numbers of white blood cells increase.[6]

Studies have shown that the application of wet heat to the forearm for a period of twenty to thirty minutes at a temperature of 113° doubled the rate of blood flow which persisted beyond the termination of the treatment for an hour.[7] He further reported that the penetration of these intense applications of moist heat was as much as 3.4 centimeters to reach the superficial muscle layer.[8]

Since we know that the peripheral resistance in the small vessels, such as the arterioles, has such a profound effect on blood pressure control, it makes a lot of sense to make use of the various thermal hydrotherapeutic procedures as a means of dilating the blood vessels close to the body surfaces. The effect of these applications would therefore be a significant additional procedure for reducing the blood pressure.

The skin has specific areas overlying the various organs which are related to the internal organs (or viscera). Thermal applications to these skin areas may thus influence activity in a specific organ system as well.

Blood pressure is a factor of the blood volume multiplied by resistance of the blood itself and the arteriolar resistance. By increasing the rate of blood flow and decreasing the peripheral resistance through thermal hydrotherapeutic procedures, one can alter the blood pressure, our ultimate goal.

Here are some reflex responses:

1. Prolonged heat to the anterior chest will increase the heart rate, decrease its force, and lower the blood pressure.
2. Prolonged moist heat over the kidneys in the back and over the lower abdomen in front will increase the production of urine (hypertensive patients have an excess amount of salt and fluid volume).
3. An ice bag applied to the anterior chest slows the heart rate and increases its blood volume pumped with each beat.[9]

The application of Kenny packs (by Krusen and Wakim) demonstrated significant increases in blood flow to all four extremities. An increase in local tissue metabolism occurred and the metabolites produced aided in local vasodilatation of the blood vessels by direct chemical effect.[10]

When using the terms "hot" or "cold," it is important to relate these to body temperature (98.6°). If the temperature is above body temperature, it is called warm or hot. If it is below body temperature, it is called cool or cold. Here is a suggested reference:

Very hot	140° and above
Hot	100° to 104°
Warm	92° to 100°
Tepid	80° to 92°
Cool	70° to 80°
Cold	55° to 70°
Very Cold	32° to 55°[11]

The speed of chemical reactions increases two to three

times for each 10° rise in temperature.[12] The need for a water thermometer is essential.

Healing Waters

Now there is at Jerusalem by the sheep market a pool, which is called in the Hebrew tongue Bethesda, having five porches. In these lay a great multitude of impotent folk, of blind, halt, withered, waiting for the moving of the water. For an angel went down at a certain season into the pool, and troubled the water. Whosoever then first after the troubling of the water stepped in was made whole of whatsoever disease he had (John 5:2-4).

For thousands of years water has been associated with healing. No wonder the Hot Springs National Park was built around the concept of healing water. There are some twenty hydrotherapeutic institutions, all under Federal regulation, built at this site.[13]

Many have lost the concept of why the water was used in the first place. The typical spas today frequently omit the water phase altogether, missing the advantages the healing waters are able to bring. I would encourage you to consider the advice of a certain servant who once counseled his enraged master, Naaman, after being told to go dip in the Jordan, "If the prophet had bid thee do some great thing, wouldest thou not have done it?" (2 Kings 5:13)

The Properties of Water

It is important to understand the physiological properties of water in its use as a therapeutic agent.

- Water can both absorb and emit large quantities of heat.

- When water is vaporized (changed from fluid state to vapor), 540 calories of heat are required for each gram of water vaporized. There are approximately thirty grams of water in each ounce. The result is a dramatic cooling effect to the skin.

- When water is changed from vapor or steam back to its fluid state, 540 calories are released. This is sufficient to cause burns if the skin should come in contact with it.

- When water changes from fluid to solid (ice), 80 calories of heat are released in the process per gram of water. These same 80 calories are required to melt one gram of ice, thus making ice an effective cooling agent when applied to the skin.[14]

Since water exists in three phases — solid, liquid, and vapor — in a fairly narrow range of temperatures, it can easily be used therapeutically.

Ice is effective as a cooling agent. Short applications result in stimulation. Longer applications depress various functions; thus the rationale of cooling a patient by the use of hypothermia in preparation for certain surgeries and to slow metabolism.

As a liquid, water is useful for various baths, changing body temperature levels.

As a vapor, it is useful in inhalation, steam baths, and to produce sweating and lowering of blood pressure.

Seldom do people think of water as an agent for health promotion in modern day America, but this useful health promoting aid has too long been overlooked. The steam bath should not be forgotten, particularly when one thinks of non-pharmacological methods for lowering blood pressure.

In times of stress or agitation, when the blood pressure soars and emotions run rampant, how useful to employ a simple hydrotherapeutic procedure right in the home to reduce tension, to relax, and assist in the restoration of normalcy. Its cost is nearly negligible.

Method

1. Drink eight to ten glasses of water daily during this program.

2. Learn what hydrotherapeutic procedures work for you.

3. Practice one hydrotherapeutic procedure daily to relax and invigorate you.

4. A hot pack applied to the chest over the heart increases the heart rate, decreases its force, and lowers blood pressure.

5. An arm bath (mid-biceps) beginning at 96° and gradually increasing to 113° over a period of ten minutes can increase the circulation markedly and lower the blood pressure.

6. A hot foot bath can increase the amount of water and salt excreted from the body, and thereby lower the pressure. (Not recommended for diabetics or those with circulatory problems.)

7. The "contrast bath" is a powerful procedure for the body, and involves a hot or steam bath followed by a cold application. It generally promotes rapid breathing and is found useful to the blood vessel tone.

8. Take your blood pressure before and after each procedure.

9. It is best that these procedures be done in the presence of a therapist, particularly if one is middle-aged or older.

Nicotine and Caffeine

Goals

- Stop smoking as soon as possible
- Reduce or omit caffeinated beverages

Science Deals With the Measurable

One cigarette raised systolic blood pressure by some 20 mm Hg in a pregnant female, even thirty minutes after smoking the cigarette.

—The Feminine Mistake

When non-coffee drinkers were given two or three cups of coffee, their blood pressure rose 14 mm Hg systolic, and 10 mm Hg diastolic one hour after ingestion.

—Management of Essential Hypertension

Discussion and Rationale

Smoking

In the film *The Feminine Mistake*, a woman is shown smoking during her pregnancy. She is allowed to view the effects of one cigarette on the blood vessels of her hand and the consequences to her unborn baby. The effect of smoking one cigarette on her blood vessels and on the baby is dramatic. The vessels in the hand practically disappear due to vasoconstriction (narrowing of the vessel walls) to the point of nearly eclipsing blood supply.[1]

Also in this film, the blood pressure is taken under regular conditions and then repeated after smoking one cigarette. The rise in blood pressure is surprisingly high: 22 mm Hg.

We know that deaths from hypertension are more common among smokers, and that smokers have a higher frequency of malignant or accelerated hypertension. A greater incidence of cerebral (subarachnoid) hemorrhage also occurs among the smoking population.[2]

In a recent article in the *Washington Post*, the writer observed, "No health official can fail to see that tobacco and alcohol are bad for our population."[3]

Few subjects have been researched as much as the relationship between smoking and health. The evidence is so overwhelming that one finds this conclusion near impossible to escape: Smoking has serious adverse effects on health. It promotes cancer, emphysema, heart disease, arteriosclerosis, and is associated with the worsening of hypertension.

A recent Center for Disease Control study blames smoking for 16 percent of all United States deaths in 1985. This translates into 314,000 deaths due to cigarette smoking. Put another way, a country the size of Luxembourg would be dropped from the world every year purely due to cigarettes. This means that smoking causes more premature deaths than alcohol and drugs combined, so the Center for Disease Control observed.[4]

The good news is, you can kick the habit. The social climate often influences people and their ability to stop smoking. Many people were shown to have stopped during the late sixties when anti-smoking public service announcements were televised. When these announcements were discontinued, smoking cessation rates dropped significantly and remained low until anti-smoking attitudes became prevalent again in the late seventies.

In a study of 2280 men, 95 percent of quitters did so on their own. Older men and those who smoked less than one pack a day were more likely to quit.[5]

One interesting finding of the American Health Foundation was that the longer a smoker waited between waking and smoking the first cigarette of the day, the greater the likelihood he or she would eventually quit. The quit rate was 37.7 percent for men who waited less than fifteen minutes, and 62 percent for those who could wait an hour or more. For women, the rates were 30.5 percent for the less-than-fifteen-minute group and 59.7 percent in the one hour or more quitters. Apparently, the degree of habituation has an influence on the timing of the first cigarette, which in turn influences the ability to quit.[6]

Strong advice from physicians to stop smoking has been shown to double the rate of cessation of smoking.

Frankly stated, knowing what we know today, smoking is stupid.

Passive Smoking (Non-Smokers)

An area of growing concern is that of the passive or involuntary smoker. The non-smoker is injured more by this involuntary smoke than by other environmental agents that are already regulated.

Biochemical markers studied in England and Japan showed that the particles of tobacco smoke non-smokers inhale when around smokers were equivalent to between 0.1 of one cigarette per day and two cigarettes per day. The risk of lung cancer caused by environmental smoke was positively associated, increasing the chances by 20 to 50 percent or more.[7]

Former Surgeon General of the United States Dr. C. Everett Koop reported an increase in lung cancer risk among non-smokers. Thirteen studies taken from a variety of countries have linked environmental tobacco smoke exposure to non-smokers' lung cancer risk, with eleven of these studies demonstrating a positive correlation for increase in lung cancer risk for the exposed non-smoker.[8]

Caffeinated Beverages

When a patient has an irregularly beating heart, caffeinated beverages may be at fault. The American College of Cardiology reported that in the amounts consumed by regular coffee drinkers, caffeine can cause significant and potentially life-threatening arrhythmias, particularly in patients at high risk for sudden death.

There was higher risk of death due to coronary heart disease or heart attack among men who drank six or more cups of coffee per day.[9]

When caffeine is combined with stress, the effects are additive. When patients were given a mental arithmetic exercise after an initial response to caffeine was recorded, systolic pressures increased on the average about 6.7 mm Hg.[10]

Men who drink at least five cups of coffee daily may increase their risk of a heart attack at least twofold, according to Dr. Lynn Rosenberg and associates at the Boston University School of Medicine. In a study of 1873 men, those who drank one or two cups daily of caffeinated coffee had an estimated 40 percent increased risk of heart attack. Those who drank three to four cups daily showed a 60 percent risk increase, and five cups or more appeared to increase their risk by 120 percent.[11]

Smoking and Caffeine: A Losing Combination

When cigarette smoking is combined with caffeine, the impact on accelerated hypertension is greater than either of the factors alone. A study group smoked a mean of twenty-five cigarettes per day and consumed a daily mean of seven cups of tea and five cups of coffee. Their initial blood pressure at the outset was 240/144 mm Hg over ninety minutes. Combined cigarette smoking and coffee drinking raised the pressure 14.1 mm Hg on the average. One patient had a rise of 40/30 mm Hg on coffee and cigarettes. Importantly, these effects occurred even though the patient was being treated with an average of three drugs, according to Dr. Stephen Freestone.[12]

Apparently, coffee or cigarettes taken alone do not have the same demonstrated untoward effect as the combined usage, but other spinoffs such as lung cancer and heart attacks have implications beyond blood pressure and demand our serious attention.

It is important to reflect upon the long-term results such habits will have on us and act appropriately.

Method

1. Determine that you will take control of yourself.

2. Join a program that fits your personality to help you kick the habit of cigarette, pipe or cigar smoking, or tobacco chewing.

3. Drink eight to ten glasses of water each day to help flush the nicotine out of your system.

4. Avoid other stimulants: highly spiced foods, coffee and teas, colas and alcohol.

5. Pray for God's help! More than 300,000 Americans die each year from smoking tobacco. It can destroy you before your time.

6. Increasing your outdoor exercise often helps minimize withdrawal symptoms.

7. Avoid favorite spots which are likely to increase the craving to smoke. Stay away from smoke-filled rooms which can make the temptation overwhelming.

8. Chew sugarfree gum as an alternative to having a cigarette.

9. Try decaffeinated beverages and herb teas.

10. Make use of the hydrotherapeutic procedures described in Step V.

Happiness and Self-Esteem

Goals

- Take time for a good laugh every day
- Build a healthy self-esteem

Equipment

- A humorous book or television show
- A visit to the park to relax

Science Deals With the Measurable

Systolic pressures were found to be lower during periods of happiness.

—*Internal Medicine News*

Discussion and Rationale

What is life, if, full of care,
We have no time to stand and stare,

No time to stand beneath the boughs
And stare as long as sheep or cows,

No time to see, when woods we pass
Where squirrels hide their nuts in grass,

No time to see, in broad daylight
Streams full of stars, like skies at night

No time to turn at Beauty's glance,
And watch her feet, how they can dance,

No time to wait till her mouth can
Enrich that smile her eyes began.

A poor life this, if full of care
We have no time to stand and stare.[1]

A recent published report by Dr. Gary D. James and associates at Cornell University's New York Hospital demonstrated that emotions appear to have a significant effect on blood pressure levels. Systolic pressures were found to be lower during periods of happiness. When one became anxious or uptight, apparently diastolic pressures rose to higher levels. Feelings of happiness were associated with the lowest readings while anxiety was demonstrated in association with the greatest increases in blood pressure.[2]

"There have been increased levels of hostility reported among young adult Americans who exhibit Type A behavior. These negative emotions are related to an elevation of plasma total cholesterol and low-density lipoprotein (LDL) cholesterol, the unfavorable fraction," say Gerdi Weidner, Ph.D., of Oregon Health Sciences University, and her associates. She states:

It is serious enough that such results indicate that this hostility level among people with Type A behavior may be an important factor in predicting mortality from coronary heart disease.

Overly competitive and active Type A individuals tend to exhibit a basic mistrust of others. They tend to spend an inordinate amount of time in an aroused and attentive state.[3]

Dr. Lee Berk, immunologist and researcher at Loma Linda University in California, gives further support to the concept that laughter reduces the immune suppressors, epinephrine and cortisol, which tend to block recovery. Laughter tends to boost the immune mechanisms which enhance the production of beta-endorphins.[4]

A good laugh has been known to increase the heart rate, raise blood pressure, speed breathing, and increase oxygen consumption. Subsequently, the breathing and heart rate slow down even below levels of normal, blood pressure drops, and muscles relax their tension.[5]

Norman Cousins, in his book *The Anatomy of an Illness,* explored the value of laughter in helping him recover from a serious disease which had gripped him.[6] His observations have opened many minds to the benefits of a merry heart, as advocated by the wise man Solomon: "A merry heart doeth good like a medicine" (Proverbs 17:22).

Anxiety and Its Effects

Anxiety is a consequence of life stresses which are perceived through the brain's perception and interpretation of the environment as being greater than the person's power to cope with the stress.

Many people think that the anxiety which one experiences is often subsequent to the disease one finds has overtaken him. Seldom do people think of the fact that the anxiety reaction is part and parcel of the disease. Anxiety more often contributes to a disease rather than being a result of one.

The entire body is involved in the response to stress. Though no organ system is more sensitive than another, the organ manifesting the disease is related to one's own biological propensities. Dr. Richard Rahe reported that those patients who had a propensity for gastrointestinal problems develop, under stress, the symptoms related to that organ system. In his article on anxiety and physical illness, he points out that cancer patients often experience anxiety, and hypertensive patients appear to "exhibit a combination of anger and anxiety, with patients suppressing their feelings by holding their anger in."[7]

One can even predict a person's likelihood of developing an illness in the future on the basis of standardized evaluations of stress. Those patients scheduled for heart surgery who have the highest anxiety levels before surgery tend to have the most difficulties in surgery. Cancer patients who receive chemotherapy also have pretreatment anxiety levels associated with treatment outcomes. Those with the lowest level of anxiety in the pretreatment phase had the highest treatment gain with therapy. American prisoners of war have had increased illness rates for infections, cardiac, degenerative and psychiatric disorders during the twenty-five to thirty years following their imprisonment.[8]

Happiness Is . . .

In the Duke University Longitudinal Study of Aging over a twenty- to twenty-four year period, subjects were examined periodically for physical, psychological, and social qualities. The researchers found that it took only a few key factors to predict longevity. From this data one could actually separate long-livers from short-livers. Surprisingly, these predictors proved to be 30 percent more accurate in pinpointing years of life remaining than the life expectancy predictions of actuarial tables. The factors of greatest importance were four in number. In order of rank they were:

1. Work Satisfaction—Feeling useful and the ability to hold a meaningful role in society
2. Happiness—General satisfaction with one's life situation
3. Good Physical Functioning—Probably thought to be most important by many
4. Non-Smoking

Notice that happiness ranked second only to job satisfaction, and was in fact superior to physical functioning in the line-up.[9]

How important for the hypertensive to sit down and strategize on the question of getting real happiness out of life. I personally believe, and have seen it true among countless others, that a right relationship with God through Jesus Christ

is the all-important spiritual basis for any human happiness
and satisfaction.

Happiness is closely associated with peace of mind. Peace
of mind is, in turn, associated with the absence of guilt. The
mind is not at ease until this guilt has been appropriately
addressed and, if possible, resolved. I am reminded of the lines
in a familiar hymn:

> The peace of God makes fresh my heart,
> A fountain ever springing.
> All things are mine since I am His—
> How can I keep from singing?[10]

Appendix C presents information that can help anyone be
assured of a right relationship with God.

. . . a Warm Puppy

Sufferers of hypertension may want to consider getting a
pet. Research has shown that contact with pets has a positive
effect on high blood pressure. It can reduce heart rate and blood
pressure, lessening the risks of heart disease in susceptible
individuals.[11] Dogs are great walking partners, too.

At a recent Rotary Club meeting the presenter discussed
the value of contact with pets for elderly people, particularly
those confined in nursing homes. One old gentleman who was
no longer able to talk would fill up with emotion following the
weekly visits with pets in his convalescent center. Thinking
that it made him too sad, the person bringing the animals
considered stopping the visits until she later learned that this
old man had operated a kennel in his younger days. This man
had loved his work, and visits with the animals brought back
old pleasant memories. Loving a pet can change your outlook
on life.

. . . Stopping and Smelling the Roses

I got inspiration out of one person's reflection on life. She
said something like this:

> If I had my life to live over, I would relax, I would limber
> up, I would be sillier than I've been on this trip. I would take
> more chances, and go on more trips. I would even climb more

mountains, swim more rivers. I'd watch more sunsets. I'd pick more daisies.[12]

Part of being happy seems to involve the assignment of time and priorities. Many are caught up in so many activities that they hardly have time to enjoy living. Take a moment to consider this essay written by a West Hartford third-grader in response to a school assignment:

What Is a Grandma?

A grandmother is a lady who has no children of her own. She likes other people's little girls. A grandfather is a man grand-mother. He goes for walks with the boys, and they talk about fishing, and tractors, and things like that.

Grandmothers don't have to do anything except be there. They're old, so they should not play hard, or run. They drive us to the market where the pretend horse is, and have lots of dimes.

When they take us for walks they slow down past things like pretty leaves and caterpillars, and they don't yell "Hurry up!"

Usually they are fat, but not too fat to tie your shoes. They wear glasses and funny underwear. They can take their teeth out. They aren't real smart, but they can answer questions like, "Why do dogs chase cats?" and "How come God isn't married?"

Everybody should try to have a grandma, especially if you don't have a TV, because grandmas are the only grownups who have time.

Self-Esteem

How do you feel about yourself? When you consider others, maybe even your peers, do you consciously compare yourself? Does this factor have any bearing on your response to a lifestyle program?

Dr. Rudolf Zacest reported at the Third European Meeting on Hypertension his findings regarding persons with low ego strength. It has been demonstrated that those persons with circulatory complaints and/or low ego strength are most likely to drop out of a lifestyle modification program for high blood pressure control. These two factors were consistently associated with the highest dropout levels—59 percent for circulatory complications and 56 percent for low ego strength. [13]

Those persons with both complaints had an 89 percent failure rate.

We want to help bolster your self-esteem during this program to help you succeed. Work with us on building ego strength and character.[14]

Method

1. Avoid discussions and situations that you know will lead to tension or irritation.
2. Take a casual, leisurely walk outdoors, away from the hustle and bustle.
3. Lighten up—laugh at yourself and at circumstances that normally upset you.
4. Try to look on the lighter side and associate with happy people.
5. Smile—even when you're alone.
6. Stay away from TV programs involving murders, crimes and violence. Instead, tune in humor and music.
7. Work on building your self-esteem. A good place to start is reading *His Image . . . My Image* by Josh McDowell (available at your local Christian bookstore).

Step VIII

Eating
From the Land

Goal

- During the fifteen-day program, try eating only from the menu listed in Appendix A (a non-flesh, cholesterol-free diet)

Equipment

- Plus Fifteen Menus (see Appendix A)

Science Deals With the Measurable

Rouse studied the effects of a vegetarian diet on blood pressure reduction. This diet included milk products and eggs. . . . He obtained a 7 mm Hg lowering of systolic pressure and a 3 mm Hg lowering of diastolic pressure.

— The Lancet

Discussion and Rationale

When a plant diet consisting of fruits, grains, nuts and vegetables was fed to volunteers and was supplemented with eggs and milk over a period of six weeks, there was a significant decrease in systolic and diastolic pressures as compared to a control group who received a typical flesh diet. The volunteers' blood pressure readings also improved over their own readings taken before the experimental diet was inaugurated.[1]

On the basis of current evidence, there appears to be little doubt that vegetarians have lower blood pressures and are less likely than meat eaters to develop hypertension.[2]

Nutritionist Ella May Stoneburner, a friend and associate of mine, wrote a letter to the monastery of the Holy Protection of the Blessed Virgin Mary regarding the vegetarian lifestyle of the Trappist monks.

Abbot George Burke's reasons for vegetarianism among the monks are worth consideration:

From the most ancient times, it was the tradition that monks would never eat meat. This was based on three reasons:

1. Meat was in no way needed in the human diet; therefore, it was a luxury.

2. Since the spiritual ideal should be to return to the state of Adam before his fall, the monks were counseled not to eat meat—something which was only done after the fall of man.

3. It is an act of supreme selfishness to kill another living being for one's own gratification—and a needless one, at that. Also, man was put on this earth to foster and to nurture it on the behalf of God, not to tear it apart and get "enjoyment" out of it. Therefore, living at peace with all things, it was considered that monks could never kill any living creature.

In addition to this, there came to be added a fourth point: The diet affects greatly a person's mental condition, and meat eating tends to make the mind "heavy;" and therefore, not consistent with an intense life of prayer and spiritual discipline. This latter point has mostly prevailed in later centuries, and is the more ordinary reason given for the abstinence from meat.

Many of our habit patterns regarding food and food

choices are largely based upon learned customs, not nutritional requirements:

> Americans are meat eaters by tradition. Yet statistics show that vegetarians in this country are thinner, in better health, with lower blood cholesterol than their flesh-eating fellow citizens. They may even live longer.[3]

Studies of the jaw structure of man place him in the group of animals that subsist on plant foods (fruit, grains, nuts, and vegetables). Man does not have the type of tooth structure that is common to those meat-eating animals such as the lion and the tiger. Instead, there is a highly developed grinder-type posterior tooth pattern that is specifically needed to chew plant food. The primates, such as the ape and monkey, who are similar in structure to man, subsist on plant foods as their major dietary source.[4]

The length of the digestive tract is also a clue to the natural selection of diet for man — it is created with the digestion of plant foods in mind. Dr. Julian M. Whitaker, in his book *Reversing Heart Disease*, compares the hydrochloric acid in the stomach of meat-eating animals with that of man, suggesting that there is a twenty-fold difference between that of the meat-eating mammals and man. Such large amounts of acid are necessary for the rapid digestion of flesh food. Plant foods do not require such amounts of hydrochloric acid nor is the short intestine suitable.[5]

Large populations of the world have lived for centuries on diets considered near-vegetarian because of economic necessity and availability of little or no animal products. Today, however, in an affluent society where food supplies are abundant, an interesting trend has been developing. More and more Americans, particularly young adults, are becoming vegetarians.

As the world's animal protein supply dwindles in relationship to population, vegetable protein products will supplement and extend existing protein sources.

A number of misconceptions about vegetarianism need to be corrected. One is that we need meat for strength. However, "yaks don't eat it, elephants never touch it, horses wouldn't look at it, and powerful buffalo and fast-running deer all survive without it!"[6] We know that vegetarians have played in and won Olympic games, and hold significant championship records in numerous areas of athletic competition.

World Health Magazine presented an article by Ned Willard which summed it up very well:

> During the past decades, for example, evangelists of a Western way of life have, in good faith, helped spread a false gospel to the rest of the world. This included the belief that only a diet based on meat and animal products could ensure health and growth.[7]

My sister went away to college where she became infatuated with a man who ate no flesh food. I remember so well when she returned home with her newly adopted program. We teased her mercilessly and made fun of her concepts. But ultimately, I was intrigued with this "new" wrinkle. I observed the gradual and subtle way this practice entered our lifestyle. It was not long before I found myself trying some of the menus and recipes, discovering for myself how vegetarianism could be both appealing and delicious. Nearly thirty-five years have passed since that time and I have never regretted my decision to take this giant step for my health.

The Western diet designating bread as the staff of life accompanied by meat, eggs, milk, and locally available vegetables has come to be accepted as the ideal diet for mankind. But today, nutritionists everywhere in the world feel that the Western diet is too high in total energy, too high in protein, too high in fat, too high in refined sugar, too low in fiber and obviously too high in salt.

A flesh diet places the heaviest strain on the world's limited food supplies and resources. Food that could nourish people is given to animals. Even more importantly, it takes about seven times as much food to produce the same amount of energy by feeding it to an animal first than it would if consumed directly.

Consider these statistics which indicate the number of days of protein requirement produced by one acre of ground yielding selected food products. One can only speculate how far this would go in helping alleviate worldwide famine.

1. Beef cattle: 77 days of protein requirement (by a moderately active man) produced by one acre yielding food product

2. Hogs: 129 days

3. Poultry: 185 days

4. Milk: 236 days

5. Corn flakes: 354 days

6. Oatmeal: 395 days

7. Rye flour (whole): 485 days

8. Wheat flour (white): 527 days

9. Rice (white): 654 days

10. Rice (brown): 772 days

11. Corn meal: 773 days

12. Wheat flour (whole): 877 days

13. Beans, dry edible: 1,106 days

14. Peas, split: 1,785 days

15. Soybeans, edible: 2,224 days[8]

The Manufacturer's Design

We know now that vegetables alone can be combined to provide excellent protein and nutritional balance. Corn and beans, rice and beans, wheat with green peas or lentils can provide adequate proteins to satisfy human needs when eaten in adequate proportions.

A long-time friend, Dr. Eppie Hartsuker, reminisced on the classic years of the automobile in the book *The Best of Total Health*. In 1904 the Rolls Royce manufacturing company began the development of the car synonymous with luxury, wealth, and exclusiveness. These cars achieved remarkable speeds for the times and were noted for customizing the interiors to satisfy almost any taste.

There was one unique feature which I don't think any car manufacturer has since duplicated. The hood of the car was locked and the key remained in the custody of the manufacturer. Thus Rolls Royce was assured that their marvelous engines would be handled only by their own qualified technicians. Only the appropriate mechanics and shops were trusted to do the repairs.[9]

The Scriptures record the diet given by God to man in the Garden of Eden. Observe the scriptural concept regarding meat in the diet for the chosen people:

> And God said, Behold, I have given you every herb bearing seed, which is upon the face of the earth, and every tree, in the which is the fruit of a tree yielding seed; to you it shall be for meat (Genesis 1:29).

Man was not given flesh to eat in his original diet due to the fact that this would require the life of the animal. There was no death in the Garden of Eden.

During their sojourn from Egypt to Canaan, the Israelites were generally never happy with their vegetarian diet. They often complained about it. At one point God sent a very great plague among them because of their murmuring against the food that was provided:

> And the mixt multitude that was among them fell a lusting: and the children of Israel also wept again, and said, Who shall give us flesh to eat: We remember the fish, which we did eat in Egypt freely; the cucumbers, and the melons, and the leeks, and the onions, and the garlick: but now our soul is dried away: there is nothing at all, beside this manna, before our eyes. . . . Then Moses heard the people weep throughout their families, every man in the door of his tent: *and the anger of the Lord was kindled greatly* (Numbers 11:4-6,33,34).

God wanted the best for the chosen people and had selected for them the most healthful diet. The people were not happy with God's dietary selection.

And they tempted God in their heart by asking meat for their lust (Psalm 78:18).

He rained flesh also upon them as dust, and feathered fowls like as the sand of the sea. So they did eat, and were well filled: for He gave them their own desire (Psalm 78:27-32).

They soon forgot His works, they waited not for His counsel. But lusted exceedingly in the wilderness, and tempted God in the desert. And He gave them their request; but sent leanness into their soul (Psalm 106:13-15).

In another illuminating passage, the Bible compares the effect of a plant diet in the Hebrew worthies in Babylon. It is recorded that Daniel chose a diet of pulse (legumes) and water in place of the prescribed diet of the royal house, consisting of meat and wine. Fascinating was the effect seen in a period of only ten days. The result was superior health and intellectual ability (see Daniel 1).

I refer to these illustrations to demonstrate that there are reliable examples in Scripture that have given precedence to the concept of eating from the land as the practice selected by God for His people. Following this example would go far in spreading healthful nutrition today.

The *New York Times* published a startling article titled "Diet Can Heal Arteries." The patients in the study group were placed on a low-fat vegetarian diet in which less than 10 percent of calories were derived from fat, largely unsaturated in quality.[10] Their conclusion: "Lifestyle changes alone without drugs or surgery can halt or reverse atherosclerosis, a hardening of the arteries that can lead to heart attack."[11]

Following a program emphasizing the reliance on fruits, grains, nuts and vegetables, one would almost immediately reduce cholesterol problems since all of these foods are cholesterol free, reduce arterial destruction, help to normalize weight, and inevitably reduce blood pressure.

The Scriptures indicate that man was originally created to live forever. God prescribed the diet needed to accomplish this. Isn't it interesting that the way to eliminate atherosclerosis is to return to the diet the Scriptures indicate as God's original prescription?

Eating from the land makes a lot of sense. I cannot emphasize enough the significant benefits of such a lifestyle change. One will find:

1. Appropriate blood cholesterol levels more easily obtained.

2. Weight control problems minimized.

3. Decreased cancer incidence.

4. Lower protein burden on the kidneys.

5. Less arterial degeneration.

6. Lower blood pressure.

7. Significantly fewer strokes.

8. Fewer heart attacks.

9. Longer life.

10. Less hunger/famine due to the nutritional capability of more food per acre.[12]

You be the judge.

John Harvey Kellogg, the prominent physician/surgeon and inventor who revolutionized America's breakfast habits, strongly advocated an all-plant diet:

> The doctor believed that meat-eating was a major precipitating factor in diseases of the circulatory system and the kidneys, that it encouraged both high blood pressure and anemia, and that it was probably largely responsible for such diseases as cancer, diabetes, and apoplexy.[13]

He pointed out that it took 100 pounds of grain to make three pounds of beef steak.

Among his patients at the then-famous, fully vegetarian Battle Creek Sanitarium were such notables as Edgar Welch, J. C. Penney, Montgomery Ward, S. S. Kresge, Harry F. Sinclair, President William Howard Taft, William Jennings Bryan, Eddie Cantor, Jose Iturbi, Percy Grainger, Lowell Thomas, Alfred DuPont, John D. Rockefeller, and Thomas Edison.[14]

It takes a great deal of self-discipline to change to a vegetarian diet, but the change will bring rewards that are measurable in life extension. It may take time and your first attempts may result in failure, but with perseverance, you can do it.

Method

1. Make a commitment to follow the Plus Fifteen program instructions carefully and strictly.

2. Prepare foods exactly as directed. The program is cholesterol-free for fifteen days.

3. Do not alter the menu without checking first with a dietitian or your doctor.

4. The emphasis is on fruits and raw vegetables (as natural as possible) in abundance. Cooked rice is permitted as mentioned in your scheduled outline.

5. The first three days is a modified fast. This is limited to fruits and grains for cleansing and for adjusting your body to the limited program.

6. Eat only whole meal bread.

7. Eat only at meal time. No snacks.

8. Eat slowly and chew your food thoroughly.

9. Allow four to five hours between meals. No food or drink except water allowed during this period.

10. No animal fat, butter or lard, eggs or meat.

11. Egg whites and skim milk are allowed on this program.

Alcohol and Hypertension

Goals

- If you consume alcohol regularly, reduce consumption to two drinks daily
- Preferably, eliminate alcohol completely

Science Deals With the Measurable

A number of studies from the United States, United Kingdom, Sweden and Australia have all indicated a link between alcohol consumption and hypertension. These population studies indicate that the higher the range of chronic alcohol consumption, the higher the prevalence of hypertension.

—A Clinical Guide to Hypertension

Discussion and Rationale

No doubt about it. There is a certain romance associated with man's use of alcohol through the ages. Wine, women and song. We toast at weddings, anniversaries and other happy occasions. Stories are told of people requesting to be buried with their favorite brand of whiskey at their side in order to be able to greet old friends in style in the hereafter.

But many reasons people drink are not very romantic at all. A Gallup youth poll revealed that young people use alcohol mostly because of conformity and peer pressure. Also listed were an escape from the modern-day pressures of life, and the desire for kicks or a good time.[1]

It is enlightening to look at the changing pattern of beverage consumption in the United States over a period of nearly forty years. Whereas the per capita consumption of milk in 1945 was 42.1 gallons, by 1983 it had dropped to 27.3 gallons. Alcoholic beverages were consumed at a rate of 19.9 gallons per capita in 1945, and rose to 28.4 by 1983, outstripping milk as a preferred beverage.[2] Water consumption in 1945 was recorded at 67.2 gallons per capita, but dropped to 42.0 gallons by 1983. Soft drinks were second only to water at 8.5 gallons in 1945, and 40.0 gallons per capita in 1983.[3]

In 1984, for every person in the United States over the age of fourteen, the consumption of absolute alcohol was 2.65 gallons. This totals about fifty gallons of beer or twenty gallons of table wine, or more than four gallons of whiskey, gin, or vodka per person.[4]

Drinkers who consume more than fourteen drinks each day make up ten percent of the drinking population, yet they account for half of the alcohol consumed in this nation.[5]

Dr. Stephen MacMahon of the National Heart, Lung and Blood Institute reported that heavy drinkers (those who consume six or more alcoholic beverages each day) clearly demonstrate significantly greater incidence of high blood pressure over time.[6]

Other studies also confirm this association. Dr. Timothy Caris reported that population studies indicate that the higher the range of chronic alcohol consumption, the higher the prevalence of hypertension.[7]

When 491 working men, ages twenty to forty-five, were surveyed in a recent study, a correlation was found between alcohol consumption and prevalence of systolic and diastolic hypertension. One possible explanation for the findings, the author stated, is that repeated ingestion of alcohol causes hypertension.[8] The author concluded, "The importance of alcohol in the pathogenesis of essential hypertension and the value of counseling in patients to reduce alcohol intake is not sufficiently well recognized."[9]

Clear evidence is available which incriminates the intake of alcohol (as little as one to two ounces) per day as the most common cause for reversible or secondary hypertension among men.[10] Although alcohol is said to have a pressor effect which is reversible, it may ultimately lead to irreversible changes.

A perusal of case histories has revealed that heart disease, the non-coronary myocardial type, is frequently associated with alcohol consumption. It has thus become quite clear that chronic alcohol abuse is a major cause of cardiomyopathy (a dilated, ineffectively beating heart). The problem is worsened because treatment is often unsatisfactory. Total abstinence is advised to avert the outcome.[11]

Ignoring the Problem Won't Make It Go Away

Little time is spent seriously looking at the overall effect of alcohol on our society. While bits and pieces of the problem are occasionally mentioned, the general trend and the extent of the problem is seldom addressed.

Earlier this century, Americans amended the United States Constitution to prohibit the manufacture and sale of alcoholic beverages. Statistics since the repeal of Prohibition are very startling. For example, from 1989 FBI reports we learn that alcohol was involved in

- 66 percent of fatal *accidents*
- 70 percent of *murders*
- 41 percent of *assaults*
- 53 percent of *fire deaths*

- 50 percent of *rapes*
- 60 percent of *crimes against children*
- 60 percent of *child abuse*
- 56 percent of *fights and assaults in the home*
- 37 percent of *suicides*
- 55 percent of *all arrests.*[12]

There are at least thirteen million alcoholics and problem drinkers in the United States today, says the National Council on Alcoholism. Alcohol use is costing this country approximately $130 billion each year. This is far greater than all monies spent by Americans on education ($35.4 billion), and all contributions to religious, welfare, and charity organizations combined ($35.2 billion).[13]

Alcohol and Your Health

Heavy alcohol consumption is associated with a higher incidence of disease and premature death. Non-alcoholics tend to live ten to twelve years longer than alcoholics.

Nine hundred and ninety-two alcohol-drinking employees of DuPont were studied and matched by age, sex, job, etc. with a similar group of abstainers or light-drinking employees. Heavy-drinking employees sustained a higher incidence of thirteen diseases in comparison to the non-drinkers. There was an 18 percent higher rate for heart disease and a 2800 percent higher rate for cirrhosis of the liver.[14]

Dr. Jean Kilbourne, international lecturer on alcohol advertising, points out that alcohol advertising spuriously links alcohol with precisely those attributes and qualities — happiness, wealth, prestige, sophistication, success, maturity, athletic ability, virility, creativity, sexual satisfaction, and others — that the misuse of alcohol usually diminishes and destroys. In testimony before the United States Senate, Dr. Kilbourne documented numerous occasions in which alcohol advertising served to eliminate from magazines and news programs necessary discussions of alcohol's contribution to morbidity and mortality. Frank and honest public discussion and awareness are dampened and alcohol emerges as being entirely benign.[15]

In the final report of the Subcommittee on Non-pharmacologic Therapy for Detection, Evaluation, and Treatment of High Blood Pressure, various approaches to the control of high blood pressure with drugs were reviewed. The authors felt only three of those approaches presented warranted recommendation for their impact on high blood pressure:

- Weight control

- Alcohol restriction

- Modification of salt intake[16]

The *Washington Post* stated it loud and clear: "Any public health official can see drinking is bad for a population."[17]

Method

1. Consume your eight to ten glasses of water each day, and do it religiously. Your desire for any other drinks will diminish considerably.

2. Avoid high intake of stimulants, condiments and soft drinks during the fifteen days. This will greatly help you avoid a dependence on alcohol.

3. Pray for strength to meet temptation to drink excessively.

4. Replace the desire for drink with other items, such as the more harmless herb teas and the cereal beverages.

5. The higher the intake of alcohol per day, the greater the effect on the elevation of blood pressure. Try to eliminate as much alcohol as possible from your routine.

6. Turn your will over to God and ask Him to help you to be a complete overcomer.

7. Avoid the association of friends who will press you to drink with them.

8. Get the alcohol out of your house and/or work place.

9. Replace your usual drinking time with a brisk walk.

Which Fat Should I Choose?

Goal

- Substitute olive oil in the diet as the major source of oil for general usage

Equipment

- Olive oil for salads
- Plain olive oil (as purchased in any market)
- Creme de Vie (a skin cream)

Science Deals With the Measurable

For every gram of monounsaturated fat eaten as olive oil per one thousand calories, the diastolic pressure was reduced by half a point.

—Tufts University Diet and Nutrition Letter

Discussion and Rationale

Clear evidence is presently available that reduction in blood cholesterol will slow, or even reverse, the development of atherosclerosis. High cholesterol levels, high blood pressure, and tobacco smoking are all implicated in worsening the process, thus hastening the arterial degeneration. You may have heard the adage, "You are as old as your arteries." There's a lot of truth to that statement.

Recent breakthroughs have suggested that dietary alteration is a powerful attack on this problem. There has also been reliable research suggesting that lifestyle shift alone may stem the rapid progression of this dread complication.[1]

In the counsel and instruction given the chosen people in the Old Testament Scriptures, they were told, "It shall be a perpetual statute for your generations throughout all your dwellings, that ye eat neither fat nor blood" (Leviticus 3:17). Heeding this powerful injunction would largely reduce the problem of arterial degeneration so prevalent today.

Scientists have known for a long time that people in the Mediterranean region have lesser amounts of heart disease compared to the people of northern Europe and North America. Recent evidence has suggested that this may be due in part to the use of monounsaturated fatty acids in the olive oil commonly consumed by the Mediterranean peoples. Until recently, it was thought that monounsaturated oils such as olive oil had no effect on coronary illness. But evidence is mounting that olive oil may reduce blood levels of the low density lipoprotein fraction of the cholesterol (the unfavorable fraction — LDL) while keeping constant the levels of high density lipoprotein fraction (HDL).[2]

Importantly, it has also been demonstrated that olive oil may lower blood pressure in the hypertensive.[3]

A study by Ronald P. Mensink at Agricultural University (Wageningen, Netherlands) compared a diet high in olive oil with a diet high in carbohydrates and low in fat. The olive oil diet demonstrated a lowering of the blood pressure level as well as the diet that was high in carbohydrates and low in fat.[4]

In a study done at the Stanford Center for Research in

Disease Prevention in California, scientists found that volunteers who ate an amount of olive oil equivalent to four teaspoonsful per one thousand calories had systolic blood pressures of about 115 mm Hg. However, those who consumed an additional four teaspoonsful for the second thousand calories had blood pressure readings of 100 mm Hg, a full fifteen points lower. Even those volunteers who took in six teaspoonsful for every thousand calories eaten had systolic readings below 115 mm Hg. They reported that these findings held true even after accounting for ages, physical activity, number of cigarettes smoked each day, stress, and the amount of protein, carbohydrates, saturated fat, and alcohol consumed.[5]

This translates into a little less than a tablespoon of olive oil per thousand calories. A salad dressing made largely of olive oil used generously on a green salad will probably equal the amount of olive oil indicated here.

This is not a wholesale endorsement of the excessive use of olive oil in the diet. However, it is an important observation. I began instituting this program on a select group of my patients who had problems with blood pressure control, and was surprised with the results.

One gentleman had a pressure of 170/110 on no medicine. I asked him to try an olive oil regimen for two weeks. He did so and came back to see me following his experience. He apologized for having been up all night with a very upsetting family problem which he felt was sure to keep his pressure from normalizing. However, when I took his blood pressure it was 140/90. I asked him to repeat the olive oil regimen for two more weeks. He did, and in two weeks his blood pressure was still 140/90.

Of course, not all my patients got the same response. However, there was a significant change in those who followed the program as directed (for two weeks only).

The Tufts University Nutrition News Letter reported that a Dr. Stephen Fortmann found that for every gram of monounsaturated fat (olive oil) eaten per one thousand calories, the diastolic reading was reduced by half a point. This would mean that a person with a diastolic blood pressure of 73 mm Hg who uses ten grams of monounsaturated fat per one thousand calories might be able to lower his diastolic four points (to 69 mm Hg) should he up his intake by eight grams on a regular basis (eighteen grams per one thousand calories).[6]

From Milan, Italy, Dr. Sirtori of the University of Milan observed that olive oil improved atherogenic risk index (an arterial degeneration risk measurement) more markedly than corn oil alone.[7]

All Fats Are Not Created Equal

A diet rich in animal fat has been linked to certain types of cancers, including cancer of the breast, prostate, ovary and colon. There has been a link between meat consumption and colon cancer as well as between fatty diets and three endocrine cancers.[8] It further has been shown that animal fat, especially in meat and milk, increases the risk of certain cancers and that vegetable fat does not.[9] There was a strong association with meat and milk consumption and breast cancer in women over fifty-five years of age, which was not noted with vegetable fat.[10]

Dr. Bonanome, professor of medicine and biochemistry and director of the Center for Human Nutrition at the University of Texas Health Science Center in Dallas, said:

> We now believe that excessive intake of polyunsaturated fat might not be safe. These fats do lower plasma cholesterol and especially the LDL fraction, the dangerous fraction causing atherosclerosis. But there are experimental data in animal models which suggest that excessive intake in polyunsaturated fat might enhance the risk of cancer and also might suppress the immune system. Lastly, excessive intake might increase the risk of gallstone formation.[11]

While it is difficult to generalize, it seems reasonable to point out that recent research has resulted in altered dietary recommendations by the American Heart Association. They now suggest that the intake of polyunsaturated fats should not exceed 10 percent of the dietary calories, along with 10 percent in saturated fats and the rest of the fat content of the diet in monounsaturated fats.[12]

Olive Oil as a Lifestyle Change

Dr. William Castelli, medical director of the Framingham

Heart Study, mentioned in a report in *Cardiovascular News* that "we have examples of societies that have eaten olive oil all their lives, and they don't get excesses of cancer, etc., or surprises along the way. They also tend to have fewer heart attacks, and we have a good feeling about the long-term safety of olive oil."[13]

As far back as the Exodus from Egypt, the Jewish people were familiar with the use of olive oil. It was the oil that was used to anoint kings. It was used in cosmetics and as an ingredient of the holy anointing oils. It was used to light the lamps in the holy services of the Temple as well. No adverse effects have been reported among the Jewish people through the thousands of years of its use.

There is one drawback to olive oil — it is high in calories. The consequence of obesity is one of the factors to be considered with a high intake of olive oil in the diet. You must be careful to watch the total number of dietary calories when entering such a program.[14]

Upon realizing the value of olive oil and its long-range implications, my family switched to olive oil as the major oil in our diet. We feel that with the evidence now developing in its favor and other long-term indications, it is a reasonable decision, particularly with the continuing rise of hypertension in our population. Consider olive oil as a lifestyle change for your family.

Method

1. Substitute olive oil for your present fat.

2. Avoid the use of lard or butter.

3. Use only margarine whose first listed ingredient is liquid vegetable oil.

4. Purchase the unsalted varieties when margarines or butters are used.

5. Where possible, exchange other vegetable oils with olive oil. Use olive oil in all cooking in which fat is required.

6. Refrain from the use of all foods with animal ingredients. These are sources of cholesterol.

7. Salad dressings are the source of both sodium and large amounts of fat. Be sure to use the varieties that are recommended in the program.

8. Remember the use of fats is a major health problem and is behind the overabundance of calories consumed in America today. Between 30 to 40 percent of a typical American's caloric intake is in fatty foods. In other parts of the world, where the occurrence of the degenerative diseases is low, that amount is about 10 to 20 percent.

9. Certain studies at Stanford's Center for Research in Disease Prevention suggest that olive oil itself lowers blood pressure in hypertensive patients.

10. Safflower oil, canola oil, corn oil, peanut oil, as well as other vegetable oils, are both beneficial and acceptable for general use.

Heliotherapy: Does It Work?

Goal

- Use the energy from sunlight or a sun lamp to reduce your blood pressure

Equipment

- An infra-red lamp or sun lamp
- Sunlight
- An appropriate sunscreen — PABA 29
- Eye shields

Science Deals With the Measurable

Hypertensives are more sensitive to radiation from sunlight and other sources than persons with normal blood pressure. The amount of depression of the systolic blood pressure was in the range of 2 to 41 mm Hg (average 17), and that of the diastolic pressure being 2 to 20 mm Hg (average 7).

—American Journal of Physiology

Discussion and Rationale

As far back as 1935, Dr. Henry Laurens of the Tulane University School of Medicine published articles dealing with the effects of carbon arc radiation (carbon sticks used in an arc lamp which produce incandescent light between two closely placed electrodes) on blood pressure and the output of the heart. Even then there was considerable evidence that carbon arc radiation of sufficient intensity and duration lowers blood pressure.[1]

In fact, research by the Finsen Institute demonstrated in 1905 that irradiation with a carbon arc (150 amps., 65 volts) produced a lowering of the blood pressure of normal persons by an average of 8 to 10 percent.[2]

The source of radiant energy in these experiments was the carbon arc lamp. The breakdown of the components of light from this artificial radiation source is:

Ultraviolet — 6 percent

Luminous — 50 percent

Infrared — 44 percent[3]

In some of the experiments, "C" carbons were used for the lamps in which the percentages were somewhat altered:

Ultraviolet — 9 percent

Luminous — 24 percent

Infrared — 67 percent[4]

Why is this important? Compare these figures to the components of sunlight:

Ultraviolet — 5 percent

Luminous — 40 percent

Infrared — 54 percent[5]

Technically, sunlight is electromagnetic energy released

as solar radiation. It is filtered through our atmosphere and an outer layer of ozone.[6]

In human studies, radiation intensity was varied from thirty to ninety minutes at a distance of seventy to one hundred centimeters from the light source.[7] This was found to be sufficient to cause erythema (reddening of the skin) and peeling without blistering. The amount of erythema usually reached its peak within twenty-four hours, and gradually disappeared during the course of the next three to four days. When the exposures were multiple, the redness was allowed to disappear and circulatory functions to return to normal again before the subject was irradiated the next time.

Maximal changes were evident on the first day after the irradiation in the hypertensive and on the second or third days in the normal pressure group. The most striking observation was the increase in output of the heart following irradiation.[8]

> The indirect effects of ultraviolet radiation are for the most part caused by the release of hustamine by the damaged skin cells. . . . The circulatory system shows a fall in blood pressure but an increase in red blood cells, white blood cells, and clotting proteins. . . . Ultraviolet radiation is generally not lethal to the human body, but it can kill individual tissue cells and such organisms as bacteria.[9]

In the hypertensive there were more marked and lasting changes in the systolic pressure in thirty-one of the thirty-two observations. The depression of the systolic pressure was in the range of 2 to 41 mm Hg (average 17), and the diastolic was 2 to 20 mm Hg (average 7).[10]

The response is apparently achieved due to the effect of dilatation of the blood vessels, which ultimately controls the blood pressure levels due to their effect on lessening peripheral resistance. When these vessels are dilated, the force required by the heart for pumping blood to the periphery of the body is reduced.

Though the vasodilatation produced by irradiation is considered by some to be limited to surface areas, such as skin, others reported that it extended into the internal vessels as well.

Dr. Fred B. Moor, professor of physical medicine at Loma Linda University in California, described the use of the electric light cabinet, which employs the application of heat to the body by radiant energy with the patient sitting on a chair inside a large plywood cabinet fitted with a series of electric light bulbs. In five to eight minutes they found reduction of blood pressure due to profound blood vessel dilatation following this heating.[11]

Using Sunlight for Your Health

Those who have hypertension need to think more about getting exposure during the day to the beneficial effects of the sun. It is not often that we think of using sunlight to influence our blood pressure levels. It seems ironic that after fifty years we can rediscover important concepts reported in reputable medical journals and that those concepts still have an impact on today's explosive level of knowledge and understanding. Yet, something so simple has been demonstrated to be effective against a disease that has reached epidemic proportions in our time. It is worthy of a try as an additional aid in the march against hypertension.

Sunlight, when utilized properly and in moderation, is a powerful ally. I invite you to incorporate this therapeutic regimen into your routine. For your own safety, be careful to follow the instructions precisely.

Method

1. A daily practice of exposure of the skin to sunlight for fifteen minutes is both advised and beneficial to the blood pressure. The best time of day to benefit from the healthful advantages of sunlight is at midday. Effects are greatly lessened before 9 A.M. or after 3 P.M.

2. Take your blood pressure before your sun exposure and repeat it at the conclusion of your treatment.

3. Sunscreens can protect the body against excessive absorption of ultraviolet rays and sunglasses can safeguard the eyes. Please use both. *Note:* Every 1000 foot rise in elevation results in a 4 percent increase in ultraviolet radiation exposure, underscoring a greater need for sunscreen as the altitude increases.

Less Is Better

Goals

- Aim toward reaching your ideal weight
- Follow the daily caloric limit on intake advised for you
- Pray for appetite control every day
- Avoid inactivity or other triggers that may tempt you to want to eat

Equipment

- Bathroom scale
- The Plus Fifteen Menu (Appendix A)

Science Deals With the Measurable

On the average, with each kilogram [2.2 pounds] weight loss, patients experience a 2.5 mm Hg systolic and 1.5 mm Hg diastolic drop in blood pressure.

—British Medical Journal

Discussion and Rationale

Fighting a weight problem? Relax. So are thirty-four million other Americans, by latest federal statistics. Of these overweight persons, eleven million are severely obese. The number of fat people is increasing, which may be inseparably related to our "couch potato" syndrome.[1] Even the schools report the need to enlarge the desk seats for the earlier grades because children today are broader than a generation ago.

Less Is Better

The standard measure usually referred to is the insurance company table of ideal weights for heights. The Metropolitan Life Insurance Company has estimated that for adults over thirty years of age, somewhere around 30 percent of American men and 40 percent of American women are above their ideal weight by 20 percent or more.[2]

Why is one's weight of such concern? People of certain persuasions used to think that fatness suggested health and contentment. Even in some cultures where I have lived on occasion, there is a real honest-to-goodness fattening room for women preparing for marriage since husbands in that geographic clime prefer women with a fuller figure.

Americans spend $15 billion each year purchasing weight loss programs. That's enough money to do a lot of much-needed things of nobler motivations. We spend $15 billion a year because we eat too much. One paradox, however, underscores the real illogic of the whole scenario. Women at the bottom of the economic ladder have been found to be six times more often obese than women at the top of the financial level.[3]

Obesity is a killer disease. It is associated with heart disease and heart attacks, high blood pressure, cancer, strokes, gall bladder disease, and even osteoarthritis.[4]

The *Handbook of Hypertension* puts it like this:

> Although one should always keep in mind the distinction between causation and association, the evidence to support the concept that blood pressure and body weight are positively interrelated in adult Western populations, is both overwhelming and irrefutable.[5]

Various studies have revealed that as many as 50 percent of hypertensives may also have a weight problem.[6] Studies have shown quite clearly that even small amounts of weight loss bring surprising improvements in blood pressure.[7]

Generally, medical authorities and researchers consider relative weights over 120 percent to constitute mild obesity. This simply means if you weigh 20 percent greater than your ideal weight (100 percent), you would be listed as mildly obese. Should your relative weight be 140 to 200 percent of your ideal weight, you are moderately obese. Relative weights greater than 200 percent of your ideal weight are listed as severe or "morbid" obesity.[8]

Death rates rise according to your degree of obesity. There is an excess of mortality of 35 percent of the mildly obese who have relative weights of 130 percent of the ideal amount. When relative weights are upwards to 150 percent in relation to ideal weight, the excess mortality is doubled. But those with morbid obesity (relative weights above 200 percent of the ideal weight) have as much as a ten-fold increase in death rates.[9]

If your fat distribution demonstrates an excess amount around the waist and flank, this poses a greater health hazard than fat in the thighs and buttocks. When the fat accumulation is abdominal, the risk of high blood pressure is greater. Researchers found that when the size of the waist exceeded the size of the hips and thighs, there was an associated increase in high blood pressure, hypertensive heart disease, and diabetes.

When a person has the misfortune of having two obese parents, he has an 80 percent risk of becoming obese.

How to Lose

Though weight loss programs come in every size, shape and color, they cannot guarantee that the participant will keep off the pounds. Using typically available methods for weight loss, only 20 percent of persons will lose 20 pounds and maintain the loss for more than two years. Only 5 percent will maintain a forty-pound loss. In our culture, the temptation to excessive eating is nearly overwhelming.

The key to weight control is *decision*. Without a determination to make an effort and continue making it, one will find difficulty controlling the problem.

As long as one eats more calories than one burns, the fat problem will remain. One can balance this in two ways: eating less and/or exercising more.

Learning how to make low-calorie foods both satisfying and appealing is a great step in overcoming the obesity problem. If the food choices can be directed into foods which pack a smaller calorie punch, all the better.

We've already discussed an exercise plan. If you're following it faithfully, you've taken a giant leap forward in controlling your weight.

Less Weight = Longer Life

Of great significance from the studies of aging and longevity is that the restriction of calories is a key element in prolongation of maximum life span.[10]

When one looks at the statistics on fasting and its effect on animals, the impression is jolting. The maximum lifespan of animals that ate daily and regularly was 800 days. In all groups in which the animals were fasted intermittently, lifespan rose from 1000 to 1100 days. Fat rats lived shorter lives. When one looks at cancer, the incidence in the lymphatics is much greater (by thirty times) in normally fed animals versus the incidence in restricted animals (those who periodically fasted). Spontaneous breast cancer was brought from 60 percent to 0 percent by long-term underfeeding of these animals.

Cancers, cataracts, discoloration and matting of hair, dryness of skin, kidney disease and heart disease are all less frequent in intermittently fasted animals than in regularly fed ones.[11]

Even in micro-organisms this holds true. The micro-organism Tokophyra, when allowed to feed freely, has a maximum survival of ten days. When placed on feedings only twice daily, survival increases to eighty days, an 80 percent increase.[12]

Let's translate these findings into the human experience.

Dr. Alexander Leaf of the Harvard Medical School investigated three long-living population groups. These included the Vilcabamba in the Andes Mountains in Ecuador, the Hunzas in the Karakoram Mountains of Northern Pakistan, and the Abkhasia in the Caucasus Mountains of the Soviet Union.

First of all, it is to be noted that they are all mountain people, which would probably underscore the fitness level. Secondly, look at the average daily caloric intake:

Vilcabamba	1200 calories daily
Hunzas	1923 calories daily
Abkhasia	1800 calories daily
U.S.A.	2400 calories daily[13]

This would seem to indicate that a diet of fewer calories contributes to a longer life.

Weight control is a continuing battle. One can seldom reach a place in which he can rest, thinking he has overcome. The problem is like that of the alcoholic or drug addict. It is an ongoing battle, awaiting another opportunity to exert itself anew. But you can gain control. A catchy motto that you may want to adopt sums it up so well: Less of me, oh to be.

Desirable weights for men and women, 25 years and older

Men

Height Ft. In.	Small frame	Medium frame	Large frame
5 2	128-134	131-141	138-150
5 3	130-136	133-143	140-153
5 4	132-138	135-145	142-156
5 5	134-140	137-148	144-160
5 6	136-142	139-151	146-164
5 7	138-145	142-154	149-168
5 8	140-148	145-147	152-172
5 9	142-151	148-160	155-176
5 10	144-154	151-163	158-180
5 11	146-157	154-166	161-184
6 0	149-160	157-170	164-188
6 1	152-164	160-174	168-192
6 2	155-168	164-178	172-197
6 3	158-172	167-182	176-202

Women

Height Ft. In.	Small frame	Medium frame	Large frame
4 11	103-113	111-123	120-134
5 0	104-115	113-126	122-137
5 1	106-118	115-129	125-140
5 2	108-121	118-132	128-143
5 3	111-124	121-135	131-147
5 4	114-127	124-139	134-151
5 5	117-130	127-141	137-155
5 6	120-133	130-144	140-159
5 7	123-136	133-147	143-163
5 8	126-139	136-150	146-167
5 9	129-142	139-153	149-170
5 10	132-145	142-156	152-173
5 11	135-148	145-159	155-176
6 0	138-151	148-162	158-179

Prepared by Metropolitan Life Insurance Co. Data derived primarily from Build and Blood Pressure Study, 1979, Society of Actuaries and Association of Life Insurance medical Directors of America, 1980. Weights are given in pounds in indoor clothing.

Method

1. Weigh daily without clothes or shoes and record the information.

2. For this program, the total caloric limit for the day is approximately 1200 calories.

3. With this amount of caloric intake and the Plus Fifteen walking program, the weight problem should work itself out naturally.

4. No snacking is allowed on this program. Don't cheat on yourself and defeat your purpose.

5. If overwhelmed by a desire to eat at other times, try raw carrots, cucumbers, or celery sticks for munching or sugar-free chewing gum.

6. Avoid places of temptation.

7. Pray for appetite control.

Environmental Effects

Goals

- Spend more of your leisure time in less populated areas such as parks, suburbs, or a rural atmosphere.
- Avoid intense noise levels.

Equipment

- A park

Science Deals With the Measurable

Blood pressures of urban migrants were higher than those of rural based populations.

—Journal of Hypertension

Discussion and Rationale

When the inhabitants of Easter Islands migrate to the South American continent, their rate of rise of diastolic blood pressure with age is significant. This rise is thought to be influenced by migration.[1]

Other researchers have pointed out similar occurrences with movements of peoples from the rural to the urban environment. There is a contrast between the urban and rural Africans, with a higher level of hypertension among the urban dwellers in comparison to their rural counterparts. The existence of hypertension among the rural Africans is low: 10 percent in the Zulu, 4.1 percent in Ghana, 5.9 percent in Nigeria, and 7 percent in Lesotho.[2]

When surveys of one thousand Malawi residents were performed, significantly higher systolic and diastolic blood pressures were demonstrated among the residents of Lilongwe, the capital city, than among the rural residents of the country. However, it was suggested that this higher level was related to the higher intake of salt among the peoples in the city than those in the country.[3]

In a study of the determinants of blood pressure changes due to urbanization, it was reported in the *Journal of Hypertension* that the blood pressures of migrants were higher than those of rural based populations. The higher mean pulse rate of migrants was an indication of an automatic mechanism, perhaps stress-induced and even casually related to the blood pressure rise associated with migration.

Researchers Gutman and Benson concluded that environmental factors and their intensity and duration directly influence, to a large extent, blood pressure changes on migration of rural residents to urban environments.[4]

Shapiro further postulated that environmental factors were more important than genetic factors in determining the degree of deviation from the norm in the population at large.[5]

Though it is seldom thought of in connection with high blood pressure, noise has been implicated as a contributing factor. Men exposed to higher noise levels have demonstrated a higher incidence of hypertension.[6] In a society such as ours, there is a lot of noise involved in transportation, manufacturing, and even our music. These noises are magnified in the urban setting.

Evaluate your environment and the effect it is having on you. Make any adjustments that are necessary.

Method

1. Spend time away from the city on weekends whenever possible.

2. If you are not near the country, a regular walk in a park will be therapeutic.

3. Consider moving to a less crowded area where you can get away from the hustle and bustle of urban life.

4. Make it a habit to spend time in natural surroundings — lots of grass, trees, flowers, birds, etc.

5. Think about taking a couple of weeks at a health resort or live-in health retreat to pull yourself together.

Work
and Leisure

Goal

- Evaluate the impact of your job and leisure activities on your blood pressure.

Science Deals With the Measurable

The annual incidence of hypertension in air traffic controllers was nearly six times the new cases prevalent among second-class airmen . . . This added risk is related to working at high traffic density towers and centers.

—Journal of the American Medical Association

Discussion and Rationale

Occupational choice is fascinating to me. Sometimes people choose occupations because of the urgent need for financial survival. Sometimes this choice may involve other intervening factors. I have a friend who weighs nearly three times the ideal amount for her height. She has taken a job as a receptionist with very little need to walk about or be active at all during the course of her day. Answering the telephone is her major assignment. Her occupational choice was an extension of her sedentary lifestyle.

At Stanford University, Dr. R. S. Paffenbarger did a study of Harvard graduates, separating them into three broad categories on the basis of their calculated energy expenditure: sedentary, moderately active, and active. Those listed as sedentary burned less than 500 calories weekly in their occupations. Those who were moderately active burned between 500-1999 calories per week, and the most active group was above 2000 calories per week. The differential showed a heart attack rate from the least active to the most active nearly double in amount: 7,017 per 10,000 man-years of observation for the least active to 35.3 per 10,000 for the most active.[1]

A study of death rates comparing bus drivers with bus conductors in London by professor Jeremy Morris of the British Medical Research Council revealed that conductors, actively engaged in collecting fares on both levels of the double-decker buses, had one-third less heart disease than bus drivers. Also, they had half the number of heart attacks. Dr. Julian Whitaker points out that the conductors with their constant running about, up and down stairs, was an influencing factor.[2]

Other studies have shown that postal workers who deliver mail have half the health problems as those who sort mail.

Quite compelling evidence has surfaced that certain diseases are unduly frequent in occurrence in men engaged in certain occupations. It has been alleged that the work of air traffic controllers is stressful, leading to excess illness. Studies done by Dr. Sidney Cobb of the University of Michigan and Dr. Robert M. Rose of the Boston University School of Medicine have indicated that the annual incidence of hypertension in air traffic controllers was nearly six times the new cases prevalent among second-class airmen. They concluded that air traffic controllers are at a higher risk of developing hypertension than are second-class airmen, and that "this added risk is related to working at high traffic density towers and centers."[3]

Other researchers have drawn similar conclusions: "It has been repeatedly shown in humans that exposure to a more stressful environment will produce increases in blood pressure."[4]

Certain stressful job situations are brought about by inherent personality conflicts on the job or because one is trying to fulfill demands and goals relating to someone else's needs. This is often the case in the subordinate-to-supervisor relationship. The supervisor has pressure on him which he in turn transmits to the subordinate. If the subordinate is unable to cope with the ire of the supervisor or the stress of the situation, there will be problems.

A lady came to my office and complained that she felt her high blood pressure was related to the difficulties she was experiencing with her immediate supervisor. Her blood pressure was always high even though she was on several medications for control. She requested time off for health reasons. I wrote a letter to her supervisor, and in as kind a way as possible tried to explain to him that I felt this woman needed some time away from her job situation and the high level of pressure she experienced there.

She remained off the job for three weeks. During this period her blood pressure descended to normal and remained there. When she returned to work, her pressure returned to the same high levels. Eventually we had to write a letter to her employer requiring a job change to allow her to normalize her health. When she was transferred to another situation with much less stress involved, her blood pressure readings were fine.

Recent medical studies are demonstrating a tie between occupation and diagnoses, and this important link should not be overlooked in thinking about hypertension.[5] Your occupational choice can have a great effect on your health.

Choose Your Leisure Carefully

Recently we have had the development of a new concept: "The Couch Potato." This is the person who spends his time at home relaxing in his easy chair. He seldom engages in any leisure time activity that involves real physical exertion. He simply sits, enjoys television, and munches on his favorite potato chips.

It is important that leisure time activities offer diversion. If the work one engages in is largely sedentary, it would be wise to choose active leisure pastimes. Spending after-work hours sitting in front of a television screen would be an unwise choice for one whose occupation is largely sedentary.

Occupation and leisure time activities are far too important to be ignored when considering the constellation of causation of hypertension. This part of your world must be addressed in your attempt to understand how you may have come about your present state of health.

Method

1. Reflect on your job situation.

2. Ask yourself if you are giving your life its best health in your present occupation. Think of possible alternatives.

3. Evaluate the amount of pressure on you in your job.

4. Compare pressures on you at home.

5. Try to find ways to avoid or minimize the stressful events in your life. Two books will be of help to you: *The Secret* by Bill Bright and *Finding Peace Under Pressure* by Peter Meadows (both published by Here's Life Publishers).

6. Take a few moments to choose some wise leisure activities that you enjoy. Schedule one or two of them into your off-work hours.

7. Utilize the principles that follow in Step 15 to help you handle the stresses of life.

Step XV

Spiritual Experience and Training

Goals

- Forget those things which are behind
- Contemplate the goodness of God

Equipment

- Bible
- Various inspirational books
- Appropriate music

Science Deals With the Measurable

The relaxation response appears to be a valuable adjunct to pharmacologic therapy for hypertension, and it may also be useful as a preventive measure ... A religious patient, for example, may select meditative prayer as the most appropriate method for bringing forth the relaxation response.

— The New England Journal of Medicine

Discussion and Rationale

An illuminating experience for most of us is found in a simple little exercise which we recommend everyone do for this final step in the program. Try recording the events of a typical day. Whatever you spend any time doing should be included on your list. If you're fairly typical, you'll probably list such things as:

- Sleeping
- Working
- Eating
- Exercise
- Family time
- TV
- Leisure activities
- Commuting

How you schedule your time tells a lot about your priorities. Is there any time at all devoted to spiritual reflection or meditation? Have you devoted even a fraction of your day to contemplate your life and overall direction?

Time to reflect is often time to relax as well. It allows the pressures which daily crowd in upon us to assume their proper perspective. One often finds that those little things which have only temporary importance sap our energies, while the important things escape us. Have time's pressures blurred your perspective?

In the preface to the book *Managing Your Time,* Ted Engstrom and R. Alec MacKenzie come right to the point: "Time management, in the final analysis, really gets down to management of yourself."[1]

Mind Matters

Chronic worry has been dubbed a root cause of hypertension. Textbooks written on psychosomatic medicine document this type of association.

Hans Selye observed that an effective way to remove worry is to displace it with other thoughts. He pointed out that of all the emotions, the feeling of *gratitude* is best suited for eliminating stress. Further, he suggested that the negative counterpart, the need for revenge, is the emotion most calculated to produce stress. There is a simple truth in Selye's counsel: Awakening gratitude in another is perhaps one of the best ways for assuring one's own security.[2]

It was Dr. Arnold Hutschnecker, author of *The Will To Live,* who pointed out that aging occurs according to events and our feelings toward them. One person suffers a reverse and ages overnight, it seems, while another individual struggles to overcome adversity and moves on. Protracted stress, he felt, does not give the body a chance to regenerate. The energy is constantly depleted and the organs are relentlessly used, as in a state of mobilization. Stress sustains tension and burns our energy.[3]

Attempts made to reduce stress are many and varied. Some of these have been dealt with in our step on rest and relaxation. However, we find that there are other emotions and responses tied to factors of spiritual enrichment which need further elaboration:

- Praise
- Gratitude
- Trust
- Freedom from guilt
- Outlook on life
- Spirit of forgiveness
- Unselfish attitude
- Golden Rule

In attempting to normalize our body chemistry, these areas concern us because of their impact on our long-term satisfaction with ourselves and the peaceful co-existence with our neighbors. The Golden Rule should always be our goal and will help dispel much interpersonal bitterness and unrest.

Invite God Into Your Thoughts

There is a dimension involved in illness that is often overlooked in its relationship to cause. Guilt is found to be a fruitful cause of disease the world round. It cannot be erased, even with concerted efforts at relaxation techniques, yoga or meditation.

While working as a missionary physician overseas, I encountered a patient who had a health problem for which she sought relief. After her treatment protocol had been completed and her physical signs all returned to normal, she still did not find comfort — not until she went to the shrine and sacrificed to her local gods. Her feelings of guilt were such that until this factor had been summarily dealt with, she could not have peace of mind.

We often don't realize the extensive damage guilt can do. It upsets the mind, ofttimes unconsciously, until it has been appropriately addressed.

A right relationship with God can replace any damaging emotions of guilt, bitterness or fear with His healing peace. At age twenty-two, I was stricken with a very serious cancer. The entire experience nearly devastated my hopes and dreams. I had an operation and an entire muscle had to be removed. Many days were spent in fear, but I fasted and prayed, trusting God for deliverance. He gave me an unexplainable peace through it all, and the miraculous manner in which He answered has bolstered my faith and courage through the years.

When I entered post-graduate training at the University of Edinburgh in Scotland, one doctor inquired of my health background. When I expressed the details of my tumor, a Rhabdomyosarcoma, he said, "The diagnosis must have been mistaken. You surely would have died." I explained to him that the specimen was examined by three pathological laboratories, the University of Southern California, Loma Linda University, and the Armed Forces Institute of Pathology, and all agreed on the diagnosis.

On the door to my medical office and examining room at the Nigerian hospital where I spent so many years I inscribed the words, "Prayer Changes Things." How meaningful those three simple words are even now to me.

I am reminded of the verses:

Come unto Me, all ye that labor and are heavy laden, and I will give you rest.

Take My yoke upon you, and learn of Me. For I am meek and lowly in heart: and ye shall find rest unto your souls:

For My yoke is easy and my burden is light (Matthew 11:28-30).

Many people suffering with hypertension are burden bearers who take on the heavy weight of cares that surround them. They often struggle with loads nearly impossible to bear. As I have listened to patients tell their stories, how my heart goes out to them. How I wish for them His peace. It was Jesus who asked the impotent man, "Wilt thou be made whole?" I believe this is His question of us as well, and that He wants to give us His peace if we will only call upon Him.

I am reminded of an old hymn that meant much to me during my trying days. It went something like this:

> For years in the fetters of sin I was bound.
> The world could not help me—no comfort I found.
> But now like the birds and the sunbeams of Spring
> I'm free and rejoicing—I walk with the King.
>
> O soul near despair in the lowlands of strife
> Look up and let Jesus come into your life.
> The joy of salvation to you He would bring
> Come into the sunlight and walk with the King.
>
> I walk with the King, hallelujah!
> I walk with the King, praise His name.
> No longer I roam, my soul faces home.
> I walk and I talk with the King.[4]

In the *Seminars in Medicine* of the Beth Israel Hospital, the following statement appears which sums up our attitude:

The relaxation response appears to be a valuable adjunct to pharmacologic therapy for hypertension, and it may also be useful as a preventive measure. This response can be elicited by noncultic techniques or by other methods, which some patients may prefer. A religious patient, for example, may select meditative prayer as the most appropriate method for bringing forth the relaxation response. The freedom to choose a technique that conforms to a patient's personal beliefs should enhance compliance.[5]

Decide how you're going to use your spiritual experience and training in your battle against hypertension.

Method

1. Plan a quiet time of contemplation daily in God's out-of-doors, preferably among the flowers, trees and shrubs.

2. Listen to relaxation or praise and worship tapes available from Plus Fifteen or your local Christian bookstore. Reflect upon the goodness of God during your periods of rest and relaxation.

3. Ask yourself where you are headed. Take into consideration the way you may be using your health. Think of ways to improve your health. Who can help you accomplish this better than God?

4. Study the Hebrew hygienic code in Exodus, Leviticus and Deuteronomy and try to determine what was intended for those ancient people in their health laws.

5. Adopt an attitude of gratitude and thankfulness for the many features of life that are free: spring mornings, sunsets, stars, etc.

6. Look at the principles for prolongation of life presented in Scripture and compare your lifestyle with the suggestions offered.

7. Ask yourself how you are prioritizing your time and how you might use it more effectively for your own health benefit.

8. Regularly spend a little less time with those less fortunate than yourself, offering a helping hand when you can. Your perspective on your present situation will be changed.

9. Read *The Secret: How to Live With Purpose and Power* by Dr. Bill Bright, available at Christian bookstores or from Here's Life Publishers.

Ignoring the Problem Won't Make It Go Away

Tony's brother had just died of a heart attack at age thirty. He had not been sick. He was an overweight smoker with high blood pressure. Nearly in tears, Tony explained how his grandfather had died before age sixty of a similar episode. His father had experienced minor complaints at age forty-two, which resulted in his need for triple vessel bypass surgery. The family history for heart disease was strong, and the long-term outlook grave. Tony was worried about his chances of a similar fate as his brother and grandfather.

Research scientists have known since 1913 that patients with high blood pressure die prematurely. Some researchers have even suggested that the higher the pressure, the shorter the longevity for those with pressure in the abnormal range. Those with pressures in the 140/90 millimeters of mercury range are not as likely to live as long as those with pressure in the 130/90 mm Hg.[2]

Usually in the natural course of the disease, there is a long phase in which hypertension is basically symptom-free. This is followed by a period of various organ complications. From statistics reported by insurance companies, we know that life expectancy is reduced at all ages and in both sexes when the diastolic pressure exceeds 90 mm Hg, and is sustained at this higher level over time.[3]

You ask, What are my chances if I do nothing about my high blood pressure? Statistics demonstrate that 25 percent of untreated patients with hypertension will experience a significant rise in their pressure each year.[4]

Coupled with that, an Australian study of untreated patients with mild high blood pressure revealed that 48 percent experienced significant declines without therapy over a three year period.[5]

Symptoms of High Blood Pressure

There is a close relationship between elevated arterial pressure and the development of atherosclerosis (hardening of the arteries), acceleration of atherosclerosis, and aggravation of atherosclerosis both in large and medium-sized arteries.

Untreated hypertension is associated with increased or early mortality. Life shortening may be ten to twenty years. Some thirty percent will show evidence of atherosclerosis, and fifty percent will have damage to various target organs related to the hypertensive process.[6]

A large number of patients are symptom free, which, unfortunately, tends to allow them to treat their disease more casually. This could be disastrous.

Generally speaking, the symptoms and signs which accompany complicated high blood pressure may include:

Headache. These tend to be in the back of the head and occasionally are associated with stiffness of the neck. They may be serious enough to disturb one's sleep and can even produce associated symptoms such as vomiting.

Giddiness or Lightheadedness. This may not be a major symptom, but when patients reflect on vague sensations it may be recalled. This may be related to disturbances in the vessels of the inner ear.

Personality Changes. It has been reported that persons suffering with severe forms of hypertension (accelerated varieties) may sustain changes in personality related to their disease and its effects on the vessels in the brain.

Shortness of Breath. On occasion this symptom plus chest

pain may be experienced in relationship to effects on the heart and lungs.

Heart Attack. This may be an untoward complication of sustained high blood pressure.

Congestive Heart Failure. This commonly results in a patient for whom the demands on the heart have increased to a point of no resolution. When the output of the heart cannot keep pace with the increased workload, the heart may fail.

Nosebleeds. These are not uncommon for uncontrolled high blood pressure sufferers. Bleeding occurs also at other unexpected sites as a result of the level of the blood pressure on the end organ, e.g., the eye, the kidney, the heart, or the brain.

Eye Changes. Hypertension may cause a blurring of vision and/or blind spots in the visual fields.

Urinary Frequency. This is a common manifestation of hypertension and it suggests kidney involvement. It may disappear when pressure is restored to normal range.

Minor strokes and cerebral deterioration may be manifestations of extreme vascular complications of hypertension. Extreme cases of vascular constrictions (narrowing) in the brain can produce such symptoms.[7]

What High Blood Pressure Does to the Body

It has been suggested that the average person suffering with high blood pressure goes undiagnosed and untreated approximately fifteen years. Early detection is of great importance to avoid other complications. What are these complications?

Blood Vessel Changes

When the blood pressure is persistently elevated it can cause damage to the arteries (large blood vessels) and also to the arterioles (smaller blood vessels). This damage involves a process in which the walls of the blood vessels themselves are thickened. We call this arteriosclerosis, or hardening of the arteries. When this happens, the inside opening of the artery becomes narrower, or smaller, thus causing a decrease in the amount of blood flowing through it. The result is increased blood pressure. In addition, the blood vessels within an organ affect the organ itself when they are damaged.

Heart Changes

The heart is affected by high blood pressure. When the vessels thicken and stiffen, the work of the heart to force blood through these now-changed vessels is greater, thus increasing the heart's workload. Sometimes the heart increases in size to cope with this stepped-up workload. Should the increased work demand on the heart continue to escalate, the enlarged struggling heart will reach a point in time in which it is unable to cope with the new demand. The result is heart failure or inadequate pumping action of the heart.

Brain Changes

Two hundred thousand people die in the United States each year from strokes. Strokes are due largely to obstructions in the blood vessels in and around the brain. High levels of blood pressure may cause certain blood vessels in the brain to rupture, resulting in hemorrhages in the brain tissue. This damage to the brain may result in the loss of activity in that portion of the brain affected by the hemorrhage. We see the results as a stroke, with loss of function in the extremities, loss of speech or vision, and a host of other complications depending on the area of the brain involved.[8]

Kidney Changes

In order to function at their best, the kidneys require some 20 percent of the output of the heart with each beat. When they do not receive this amount they pour out a substance which affects changes in the blood pressure. When the blood pressure is too low or the arteries unable to meet the kidney's demands, the kidneys will fail.

Eye Changes

Eye changes resulting from thickening and stiffening of blood vessels cause the vision to fail or become impaired.[9]

Does Therapy Prevent Complications?

Therapy aimed at reducing the pressure makes sense. Many of the complications are the direct result of increased amounts of mechanical force on the target organs. Reducing the pressure by whatever means — drug or physiologic — should also reduce the untoward effects on the vessels and organs not designed to withstand this level of pressure.

Published studies have adequately confirmed that, simply stated, the higher the pressure above a healthy level of 120/80 mm Hg, the shorter the life expectancy.[10] That's what one can expect if one decides not to treat this disease.

The honor of Kings
is to search out a matter (Proverbs 25:2).

9

Does Drug Therapy Cure Hypertension?

My phone rang early one morning before I had climbed out of bed. On the line was one of my patients who frequently calls inquiring about refills on her mother's blood pressure medicines. Her supply was exhausted and her mother's pressure was already up again, she reported.

The function of the antihypertensive medication is to reduce the diastolic pressure to normal levels. When physicians say that the blood pressure is under control, they simply mean the blood pressure is within normal range.

Generally speaking, when the medication is exhausted the blood pressure climbs again. This is why instruction given to hypertensive patients is for a life-long medication administration. Drug therapy does not *cure* hypertension, but seeks to *control* it.

Before entering the Plus Fifteen program, consider the following salient points:

First, if a patient refuses to alter his lifestyle or is unable to deal with the inconvenience of stopping smoking, curbing excessive drinking, reducing salt, or practicing a more active physical program, *then it would be greater wisdom to take the medications.*

Second, if after making the appropriate lifestyle alterations, one does not realize a lowering of blood pressure into a safe range, then entering into a drug control program is a sensible alternative.

Let's take a closer look at the drugs used in the treatment of high blood pressure. They fall into several major groups.

Diuretics

These are commonly referred to as "water pills." Because of their action on the kidneys, one tends to pass more urine. Large amounts of salt in the diet are associated with the development of high blood pressure in those genetically susceptible. Salt tends to hold water in the body and it is this fluid overload that is implicated in high blood pressure. Further, it has been demonstrated that blood pressure can be lowered by reducing the sodium level and disposing of the excess fluid.[1]

Diuretics were introduced to help reduce this load of salt and water and also to lower blood pressure. A combination of a diuretic and a low-salt diet has been very helpful to many patients.

When the body rids itself of some of its salt, it also decreases extracellular fluid (that is, fluid outside cells). Weight is reduced and maintained as long as the person is under treatment. However, if the volume lost is replaced, the blood pressure will rise to its previous level.[2]

No great differences exist between the various diuretics in terms of their blood pressure lowering activity.

What drugs are included in this group?

Hydrochlorothiazide	Chlorthalidone	Furosemide
Indapamide	Metolazone	Chlorothiazide
Cyclothiazide	Amiloride	Triamterene
Spironolactone[3]		

The Beta Blockers

In blood vessel walls, in the heart, and in the lungs are structures known as beta receptors. These receptors accept nerve and chemical stimuli. As a result of this stimulation, the heart may beat harder and faster. The effect on the blood vessels may be a narrowing of their size or diameter.

In some driven individuals, this class of drugs blocks the sympathetic nervous system (the "fight or flight" system of the body) by toning down the exaggerated response. These drugs also tend to slow the heart and lower the blood pressure by affecting smooth muscle in lungs, muscles, and blood vessels.

This group of drugs tends to block the part of the nervous system that produces energy and enthusiasm. This is not a side effect of their activity but rather a part of their action. They are designed to diminish vitality — the old sparkle. Among other things, sexual excitement, interest, and performance may also suffer. The pulse rate slows down as well.[4]

Benefits of using these drugs include reducing chest pain, helping to prevent migraine headaches and even reducing the risk of a repeated heart attack in certain people.

A listing of these drugs commonly used would include:

Atenolol (Tenormin)   Metoprolol (Lopressor)
Nadolol (Corgard)   Pindolol (Visken)
Propranolol (Inderal)   Timolol (Blocadren)
Labetalol (Normadyne)[5]

Vasodilators

Hydralazine (Apresoline) has been used in high blood pressure treatment for more than thirty years. Vasodilators act directly on the smooth muscle in the blood vessel walls causing them to relax or dilate. When the smooth muscle dilates, the blood vessel is less constricted, and the blood pressure goes down.

Blood pressure control is frequently exerted in the smaller arteries where narrowed vessels cause the peripheral resistance to be greater. Any procedure to lower the peripheral resistance, that is, relaxing the blood vessel wall (smooth muscle) can therefore bring about the lowering of the blood pressure. But these drugs can also worsen congestive heart failure, or precipitate angina or chest pain. They may produce a symptom complex resembling systemic Lupus Erythematosus. These drugs have also on occasion been implicated in the development of myocardial infarction or heart attack. Drugs in this group: Apresoline and Loniten.[6]

Calcium Channel Blockers

The major effect of this group of drugs is to block the entry of calcium into heart muscle and vascular smooth muscle. If calcium cannot enter the smooth muscle, the muscle cannot contract because calcium is needed to accomplish this contraction. These drugs are direct-acting blood vessel relaxers. Patients with high blood pressure often have a greater amount of blood vessel narrowing (constriction) than is usually found in a normal population. The basic effect of calcium channel blockers is to relax or dilate the smooth muscle of the blood vessels and heart.[7]

Examples:

Procardia	Isoptin
Cardene	Cardizem

Ace Inhibitors

ACE means *angiotensin converting enzyme*. The group of drugs known as ACE inhibitors block the formation of angiotensin converting enzyme. This enzyme, Angiotensin II, has a powerful effect on the blood vessels causing them to constrict or tighten, thereby increasing the blood pressure. ACE inhibitors block this action, and have been used effectively to treat high blood pressure and heart failure.

Examples:

Capoten	Lisinopril
Vasotec[8]	

Peripheral Blocking Agents

Reserpine, a drug in this category, works by depleting the body of the nerve transmitter nor-Epinephrine, a vasoconstrictor.[9] It is effective and even more so when combined with diuretics.

Central Agents

These drugs work in the lower portion of the brain to reduce the number of chemical stimuli ordinarily released into the blood. They thereby relax the blood vessels.

Many of these drugs have not been used throughout a patient's lifetime and we do not know their effects when used over an extended period of time. The longer a drug is on the market, the more likely an elaboration of its effect will become known.

Rauwalfia Serpentina is a medicinal herb from India used to treat and tranquilize the mentally disburbed. In July 1949 it was reported to be effective in treating hypertension,[10] and later confirmed by other researchers.[11]

Sympathetic Ganglion Blockers

This group of drugs acts upon the sympathetic ganglion of the autonomic nervous system; they are very powerful agents for lowering blood pressure. In this group are two drugs known as Ismelin and Hylorel.[12]

Alpha Blockers

A group of specialized cells known as alpha receptors are found in the walls of blood vessels. These receptors may influence the tightening (constriction) or loosening (dilation) of the blood vessel walls. An alpha blocker is a drug aimed at blocking the tightening effect of the alpha receptors mediated through chemical or nervous stimuli. Minipress is an example of this type of drug.[13]

Drugs do not cure high blood pressure but rather seek to control it. Is the possible liability to reactions and other interactions equivalent to their real value for a mild hypertensive?

For which of you, intending to build a tower,
sitteth not down first,
and counteth the cost? (Luke 14:28)

10

The Dollars and Sense of Blood Pressure Control

Data from the Social Security Administration clearly show a sizeable amount of disability in the labor force attributable to hypertensive disease . . . these data conclusively rank hypertensive disease and its complications at the top of the list as producers of disability for all of the major sex-race groups in the labor force.[1]

I was once approached by a beggar who asked, "Buddy, can you spare a dollar for some bread?" I remember giving the man money, but I seriously doubted it would be used for the cause for which it had been requested.

It reminded me of a text I had once read: "Much food is in the tillage of the poor: but there is that is destroyed for want of judgment" (Proverbs 13:23).

An Economic Drain of Family Finances

In contemporary America, a person may easily pay $84 monthly ($1000 per year) for pharmaceuticals to control high blood pressure. Estimates suggest this may actually be a modest figure. And this medication cost figure does not include physician visits, laboratory costs, or job-related losses from the disease. Moreover, there are additional costs for complications from high blood pressure, such as heart attacks, strokes, heart failure and arteriosclerosis.

By comparison, see what $1000 annually could accumulate if invested. If $1000 is invested each year for thirty years, it would compound to $105,681.62 at 7.62 percent, and soar to $180,943 if invested at 10 percent.[2]

It makes economic sense to focus one's attention on a more healthy lifestyle.

A Substantial Business Proposition

With nearly 60 million persons suffering from high blood pressure in the United States, the implications are staggering. Direct consumer cost for high blood pressure treatment is in the multi-billion dollar range for medication alone.

Wholesale prices for antihypertensive medication worldwide have escalated from $610 million (U.S. dollars) in 1970 to $2.8 billion in 1982 — a 450 percent increase in only twelve years. High blood pressure control is big business.[3]

Finance: A Barrier to Adequate Control

Many think the cost of medication is minor since it occurs in relatively small increments. However, for a poor family this could represent a substantial investment of their life's earnings. Dr. Neil B. Shulman, of the Emory University School of Medicine, cited the cost of antihypertensive medication as a barrier to high blood pressure control for certain patients in the state of Georgia.[4]

The cost of keeping a continuing supply of medicine was reported as a problem to as many as 50 percent of one group. In addition, more than 50 percent of respondents with moderate to severe hypertension indicated there were times when they could not afford a refill on their medication. This situation places them at risk for a rebound in blood pressure and possible kidney failure, among other complications.[5]

Other reports have demonstrated that when middle-aged black women (and others as well) perceive other family needs as more urgent, such as expenses on behalf of the children or other obligations in the family budget, the blood pressure medications may be omitted due to their cost.

The poor, the aged, and others with changing financial patterns may often find themselves in positions, due to life's vicissitudes, where they are unable to meet an unrelenting demand for the purchase of a lifelong drug supply. Such individuals will often have gaps in the regularity of medication supply and administration.

In the May 1990 issue of the magazine *Black Enterprise*, poverty was singled out as one of the most profound factors contributing to the disadvantaged. A statement was quoted from the National Research Council which highlighted a consistent finding across communities in the nation that persons of the lowest socio-economic status have higher death rates. When those in the lowest status were compared with those in the highest socio-economic level, an 80 percent higher overall mortality was found among the poor and a higher prevalence of almost every form of disease and disability. They further stated that blacks were disproportionately represented in the poorer class.[6]

During the same month, *U.S. News and World Report* included some shocking statistics regarding, "America's Wealth: Who Has It?" The wealthiest 5 percent have 53.5 percent of the wealth. The poorest 20 percent own 0.3 percent of the wealth, and the least wealthy 40 percent of the population own only 2.8 percent of the wealth.[7]

Considering the income levels of the average poor family:

- One family member with moderate hypertension represents a $1000 investment annually.

- Two family members with hypertension may represent a $1500-$2000 outlay or more.

- Three members with hypertension may represent in excess of $2000-3000/annum.

Over the years this means a considerable loss to the family.

What does that tell us? The cost of high blood pressure

control is not a minor matter. See the chart below for direct costs of medication.[8]

Cost Comparison of Competitive Anti-Hypertensives

Brand Name	Dosage		Pharmacy Cost Per Month
BETA ADRENERGIC BLOCKING AGENTS			
Inderal	40 mg	1 BID	$ 21.48
Corgard	40 mg	1 DAILY	22.86
Sectral	200 mg	1 BID	36.48
Tenormin	50 mg	1 BID	40.75
	100 mg	1 DAILY	30.52
Lopressor	50 mg	1 BID	24.20
CENTRAL SYMPATHETIC DEPRESSANTS			
Catapres	0.2 mg	1 DAILY	17.16
ALPHA ADRENERGIC BLOCKING AGENTS			
Minipress	1 mg	1 BID	22.64
ALPHA BETA BLOCKING AGENTS			
Normodyne	200 mg	1 BID	26.73
ANGIOTENSIN CONVERTING ENZYME INHIBITORS			
Capoten	25 mg	1 BID	28.25
	50 mg	1 BID	73.16
Vasotec	5 mg	1 DAILY	21.36
Prinivil	10 mg	1 DAILY	19.72
CALCIUM ANTAGONISTS			
Cardizem	60 mg	1 TID	43.58
Calan	80 mg	1 TID	32.48
	120 mg	1 TID	43.78
Procardia	10 mg	1 TID	42.27
	20 mg	1 TID	76.08

BID = twice daily; TID = three times daily

What is the solution to this problem? How can a safer approach be adopted?

A Viable Alternative

One researcher put it this way: "Unless non-pharmacological methods of blood pressure reduction are shown, in scientifically designed and statistically evaluated clinical trials, to be effective, acceptable, and safe, *the annual cost of drug treatment is likely to continue its current escalation.*"[9]

> There is clearly an urgent need, for reasons of safety, convenience and economics, to explore the feasibility of alternative strategies for blood pressure control. Non-pharmacological methods, however, will have to be subjected to the same rigorous scientific evaluation, through carefully planned and statistically analyzed clinical trials, as the more recently published drug intervention studies, before they can be recommended for general use."[10]

It seems reasonable to say this current debate concerning the management of mild hypertension will continue. Many now feel high blood pressure should be controlled by *lifestyle*. Since important issues are involved, lifestyle modification continues to be a touchy subject. Yet given government's budgetary consciousness and concern over the future of the health care industry, this is a crucial discussion today.

Plus Fifteen makes sense for countries who have significant populations suffering with this problem and no financial surpluses to cover it. In developing countries, drug costs are a major factor in foreign exchange and in the general health of the populace.

The Need for Moppers vs. The Need for Turners

Most often research money is spent for trials of potential drugs for intervention. Usually little money is set aside for research in lifestyle programs designed to improve the general health of the population.

We have become nearly totally dependent on drugs for therapy. But *blood pressure control can be achieved by non-pharmacological interventions.*[11] Only 10 percent of borderline hypertensives need medication. Others should diet, exercise, and watch their blood pressures, according to a recent article by Dr. Stevo Julius of the University of Michigan.[12] The Plus Fifteen program will help you do this, and more.

In August of 1979, I was involved in the All Africa Health Leadership conference in Nairobi, Kenya. At this session, Dr. Denis K. Burkitt, who first described the Burkitt Lymphoma and also the role of fiber in the diet as it relates to cancer, told about a group of health workers feverishly mopping a floor beneath an overflowing sink. They kept trying newer and more sophisticated mops, buckets and towels in an attempt to keep ahead of the problem, but all to no avail. They worked into the night, searching for more powerful instruments, more sensitive indicators of the problem. Finally someone thought of turning off the water tap.

Is it not now time for someone to turn off the tap rather than continue to mop at the problem? Shall we look for stronger and stronger medications to treat our accumulated ills, which continue to escalate day by day? Is the answer to our problem to place one-quarter to one-half of the U.S. population on antihypertensive medication? Or is it time to look for an alternate solution?

Where Will It End?

The problem of high blood pressure is, surprisingly, not being solved with more pills, although revenues for antihypertensive medications increase by 8 percent annually.[13] Will we soon become a nation of pill poppers, partially impotent, struggling with an already too great medication burden? Some rough estimates suggest that men and women sixty-five years of age or older are, on the average, taking eight or more pills a day.[14]

Salt Labeling

To require labeling of the quantitative salt content of foods would be a great step in tackling this problem. It makes dollars and sense to plan for health and longevity. We have only one chance on life. Should we blow it for a little salt? Would I exchange useful life for the excesses of today? Are they really worth that much to me? Surely not!

Community Activities

In terms of community control of high blood pressure, one must weigh many factors. It might be of considerable importance to have a complete cost-effectiveness analysis for the management of high blood pressure and compare it with similar data using non-pharmacological measure and then decide on priorities for a community.

Costs must include not only those for health care and drug treatment, but also the indirect costs from the loss of working capacity due to disease or premature death.

Swedish data indicated that direct health care costs amounted to 30 percent of the total cost while costs because of disease, absenteeism and long-term disability ranged upwards to 50 percent. The remaining 20 percent of health care costs were due to premature mortality.[15]

When one considers the implications of lifetime therapy, the costs of treating the medication side effects, as well as the total actual years of life gained, one can more intelligently weigh outcomes.

The problem calls for major efforts in seeking an intervention that will shift the entire blood pressure distribution curve to the left by some non-pharmacological, primary preventive approach. This might involve dietary changes, such as a decrease in calorie, fat and sodium chloride intake.[16]

Hypertension is a symptom of a larger problem and it will not go away just because we have more pills. In several isolated areas in our world, high blood pressure is rare or non-existent. People groups in these areas are generally labelled "primitive." What are they doing that you and I cannot choose to do also?

If thou wilt do that which is right . . .
I will put none of these diseases
upon thee (Exodus 15:26).

11

The Christian Advantage

Foremost among the nations of Near Eastern antiquity stood Israel with far-advanced sanitary regulations found in the Mosaic code. These early public health concepts are still a marvel today. Although the Bible was obviously not written as a medical text, scholars mention that its historical presentations, its public health laws, its preventive medicine concepts, and even its wordings grant us an abundance of information concerning the human body, diseases, injuries, cures, as well as many prophylactic and sanitary procedures. The material found in some portions of Leviticus is so factual that even the sophisticated present-day student cannot help but be amazed at the accuracy of the concepts presented.[1]

Even as late as the 18th century, hygienic provisions were quite primitive in the great European cities.[2] The Bible principles, quite clearly stated thousands of years before, could have spared the lives of large populations if they were heeded. Eventual progress in Europe in the control of its most devastating plagues was linked to an awareness of Bible principles of health and hygiene.

Hebrew Hygienic Code

The Hebrews sanitary laws were considered of such importance that Scripture includes the instructions given Moses for enforcing the codes. Some regulations involved having a person pronounced "unclean." Others required for the diseased to be put out of the camp for a period of time. There were also instances in which disobedience to health laws was on pain of death. In this case, such a prohibition would receive due respect, and the attention of the people would be focused upon issues of concern to the community where health matters are involved.[3]

The Israelites were only shortly out of slavery and were repeatedly stubborn in their willingness to accept the instructions Moses gave them. Because of the nature of contagious diseases, anyone who had been exposed to or in contact with an infected person was dealt with summarily due to the possible effect upon the larger community.

There are those in various countries who will not regard health principles or rules, but expect to be cared for when they have brought sickness upon themselves. These less conscious ones significantly impact the cost of providing health care. How should limited resources be used in such instances? Should one give instructions regarding the necessity for boiling water in areas of high contamination of drinking water and leave those who do not boil to their illness? To what extent should we hold individuals personally responsible for health care?

Is Faith Still Part of Healing?

The secular atmosphere in which we now live does not respect spiritual factors in disease.

Jesus often cited faith as the condition for healing. Consider the story of the woman who was ill who touched Him. Jesus said to her, "Daughter, be of good comfort; thy faith hath made thee whole" (Matthew 9:22).

He commended the faith of the centurion who came to Him, "I have not found so great faith, no, not in Israel" (Matthew 8:10).

Is faith, then, a condition for health and healing?

Faith is a word which may also be interpreted as trust or reliance, hope or expectation. I have a friend who wrote a book entitled, *Can God Be Trusted?* I believe, though, that the problem is not with God, but with us.

The Christian advantage is bound up in something called trust or reliance, hope and expectation. Are you willing to let God have charge of your life? Those who worry and fret generally are those who are ill at ease because they have no hope. All is bound up in their worldly circle of interests and concerns. They have failed to look beyond themselves for reliance and confidence. Even today, whether called faith, hope or trust, this element has a bearing on our health as you will later see.

As a medical doctor, I have seen many times how a patient's personal faith in God can give him the inner peace and positive outlook that is essential to health and healing, as well as to a fulfilling life in general. For a concise presentation from the Scriptures on how one can establish this kind of personal faith in God, I would encourage you to read Appendix C, "Would You Like to Know God Personally?" The principles you will read have made a significant difference in my life, and in the lives of many of my patients.

"The Right to Life"

Paul Tournier presents another thought which I like very much and want to share with you:

> Most illnesses do not, as is generally thought, come like a bolt out of the blue. The ground is prepared for years, through faulty diet, intemperance, overwork, and moral conflicts, slowly eroding the subject's vitality. And when at last the illness suddenly shows itself, it would be a most superficial medicine which treated it without going back to its remote causes, to all that I shall here call "personal problems."[4]

In a statement of Jesus to the Jews, He refers to His body as a temple: " 'Destroy this temple and in three days I will raise it up!' . . . But He spake of the temple of his body" (John 2:19-21). This is, apparently, the first reference in the Scriptures to the human body as a temple.

Paul again makes a reference to the concept in his letter to the Corinthians:

> Know ye not that ye are the temple of God, and that the

Spirit of God dwelleth in you? If a man defile the temple of God, him shall God destroy; for the temple of God is holy, which temple ye are (1 Corinthians 3:16,17).

The marginal cross-reference for *defile* in the King James Bible is the word *destroy:* "If any man *destroy* the temple of God, him shall God destroy . . . "

When one considers the counsel and injunction regarding destroying or killing life in the moral law, one automatically thinks of killing someone else. The issue of killing one's own body is generally not considered. However, there is virtue in studying the question of self-destruction in the text, "Thou shalt not kill" (Exodus 20:13).

What factors are important in deciding upon one's approach to life and health? How sacred is one's life, and to whom does it belong? Is man at liberty to destroy himself? How does the Bible deal with this subject of self-destruction?

Of course, another issue of concern involves the question of whether this destruction is done immediately or over a prolonged time period. Would the act be the same whether one does the destroying in an instant or over several years? Any known practice that is destroying the body, the temple of God, must be put away.

More than 200 of the 600 laws given to the Hebrews in the Old Testament Scriptures were health laws.[5] Considering this large body of instruction (far more than the amount one would expect to be given on the subject of health), what are the important implications?

Life is seen as a continuing gift from God. His love and care for us is so great that He has established guidelines to help us protect and strengthen our bodies. We are not able to exist on our own without His power day by day for sustenance.

Whereas ye know not what shall be on the morrow. For what is your life? It is even a vapour, that appeareth for a little time, and then vanisheth away. For that ye ought to say, If the Lord will, we shall live, and do this, or that (James 4:14,15).

Health Laws—Are They Really Operative?

In the natural sciences there are laws that govern the activities of nature. Many scientifically oriented persons can recall the Pythagorean theorem. In physics there is a law of mass density which states that "the mass density of an object is equal to the mass weight divided by the volume," and is stated in the equation form $D = M/V$. The mass density is equal to D; the mass weight equal to M; and the volume equal to V.[6]

If we look at this formula in practical terms, it would work something like this: Should a ship attempt to sail the sea, it is of utmost importance to know that if the mass density of the ship is greater than the mass density of the water, the ship will sink. The principle upon which ships sail the seas is that the volume of water that is displaced must be greater in density than that of the ship which it must support. Early shipbuilders understood this principle even though they never saw the equation.

There are certain laws relating to gases, referred to as Boyle's and Charles's laws. These laws describe natural happenings that were in existence long before such laws were described in the 17th century.[7]

God has laws which operate for the human organism. These laws operate for the good of mankind. They were established for our longevity. When they are broken or ignored, we pay the penalty.

Though premature death may not always be prevented or necessarily an indication of personal neglect, one must be sensitive to chronic habit patterns that tend to destroy or cut short an otherwise fruitful existence. Why should one die before his time?

What am I doing that, in fact, may shorten the life God has given me?

The major question, we might call it
the $64 million question, is . . . whether
aggressive treatment of risk factors delays
or prevents atherosclerosis and its sequelae.[1]

12

The Cholesterol Connection: Today's $64 Million Question

It was late in the day when I arrived at her room. She was very upset and in tears. She had been talking on the phone to her husband when suddenly her speech became garbled. Up to that point she had suffered with symptoms of high blood pressure and also episodes of chest pain. Now she was undergoing what many thousands of Americans have suffered — a stroke. And she was fully aware that something terrible was happening to her.

Strokes, heart attacks, and vascular insufficiency of the lower extremities are all part of a larger picture, a broad subdivision of a disease known as *arteriosclerosis* — hardening of the arteries. It is due to long-term fibrous tissue and cholesterol deposits on the inner surface of the arterial walls. These decrease the size of the opening in the arteries much like the sediment deposited on the inner surface of a water pipe.[2]

Arteriosclerosis is responsible for the majority of deaths in the United States and most westernized societies. One type of arteriosclerosis is *atherosclerosis,* the disorder of the larger arteries that underlies most coronary artery disease, aortic aneurysm (abnormal ballooning of the body's largest artery), and arterial disease of the lower extremities. We know that atherosclerosis is by far the leading cause of death in the United States.[3]

In largely primitive societies the arteries frequently remain clear throughout much of their adult life. This is particularly true in societies with a high level of fitness or physical exertion in the lifestyle and where a diet largely confined to plant products is typically eaten.[4]

It is also interesting that this disease is nearly absent in the animal kingdom under natural conditions. When a diet high in cholesterol and saturated fat is fed to monkeys and pigs, they will develop atherosclerosis. This condition, moreover, is rapidly reversed when the animals are returned, believe it or not, to a diet of vegetables, fruits, and cereal grains.[5]

Six Important Questions You Should Ask

1. Why is a high blood cholesterol level bad?

Recently, at the annual meeting of the American Heart Association, an eighteen-page statement endorsed by a panel of experts from the National Institutes of Health and the American Heart Association emphasized that the evidence linking elevated blood cholesterol to coronary heart disease is "overwhelming and indisputable."[6]

2. Where did I get all that cholesterol anyway?

Cholesterol is a waxy substance found in the blood stream that belongs to a group of substances known as sterols, all of which are really essential to life. Cholesterol enters our bodies largely through the foods we eat. It is commonly found in meat, dairy products, eggs and other animal products. There is *no* cholesterol in fruits, grains, nuts or any vegetables. The liver actually manufactures enough cholesterol in our bodies for our survival. If the dietary proportion is too high, the excess cholesterol begins to coat the inner lining of our arteries, leading to their destruction.[7]

3. Is there anything I can do about it?

Cholesterol belongs to a group of fatty substances called lipids. When the levels rise too high in the bloodstream, they become harmful.

Your part in the program involves changing certain dietary practices. For example, use low fat or skim milk in place of whole milk. Limit your intake of eggs and discard the yolks when using eggs in cooking since the cholesterol is limited to the yolk. Reduce your intake of meat, particularly the fatty portions. Choose vegetable oils such as the monosaturated varieties discussed earlier in this book. Eliminate butter and fat-laden desserts. Reducing the amount of saturated fat in the diet seems to be a key factor.

Increase your intake of soluble fiber foods as is found abundantly in the plant kingdom. This includes the various cereal brans, beans and other plant foods. Exercise and the elimination of smoking are two other important additions to your cholesterol lowering protocol.

4. How can my doctor help me?

There are five values which your doctor can measure in your blood:

Total Cholesterol Level (the total amount of all cholesterol in the blood). When you hear mention of a "cholesterol number," this is the number that is referred to. However, this total cholesterol can be divided into fractions. These lipo protein fractions are also very important.

Low Density Lipo Proteins (LDL). LDLs have been labeled as the real culprit in arterial destruction. LDL cholesterol along with calcium and fibrous substances make up the plaque that lines the arterial walls.

High Density Lipo Proteins (HDL). These substances are known as the favorable fraction of your cholesterol, since they act to help clear the arteries from cholesterol deposits. The higher the level of HDL, the greater the protection against arterial damage.

Total Cholesterol/HDL Ratio. If the proportion of total

cholesterol in the blood is balanced by a sufficiently high level of the high density lipo protein fraction, the result is still favorable. This ratio is a predictor of heart disease risk.

Triglycerides. These are other blood fats in contrast with the cholesterol, particularly more important to women after menopause, and they offer an index to the general fat level of the body. When this value is elevated, the cholesterol often is also high. Fortunately, this value is often quite responsive to the benefits of exercise. Cooking oils are triglycerides. Sweet breads and pastries often increase this number.

Your doctor may offer the option of medicine for lowering cholesterol. The potential cost for this may exceed $1000 per annum. All drugs have intrinsic risks and potential side effects which must be weighed before beginning such a program. Your doctor can assist you in this decision.

5. What is atherosclerosis?

A typical artery in the circulatory system of the body has three distinct layers which make up its basic composition.

The *intima* is composed of a specialized type of cell known as the endothelial cell. This cell plays a key role in the development of atherosclerotic plaque which is part of the process of obstruction of the inner arterial surface in strokes and heart attacks.

The *media* forms an external covering to the intima and is composed largely of smooth muscle cells which are accompanied by elastic fibers. The flow of blood through these arteries is partially regulated by the contraction or relaxation of these smooth muscle cells.

The outermost layer is known as the *adventitia* which is made up of a loose mixture of collagen, elastic fibers and smooth muscle cells, and which is also interspersed with vessels that nourish arteries themselves and nerves.

Damage to the lining of the intima is critical. The endothelial cells of the intima help to prevent clotting within the vessel or on its walls.[8]

Additionally, the smooth muscle cells of the vessels also

act to make use of lipids (cholesterol) and triglycerides. These lipids may be incorporated into the smooth muscle cells.

The impact of atherosclerosis is sometimes not taken seriously enough by the general public. You may be surprised at the damage it causes, even in its early stages:

(a) *Fatty streak.* The earliest lesion of atherosclerosis characterized by a proliferation of fat-filled smooth muscle cells.

(b) *Fibrous plaques.* These raised areas of the artery surface represent the most characteristic of the lesions of atherosclerosis.

(c) *Complicated lesions.* This involves the deposition of calcium with degeneration of the plaque, thrombosis and ulceration. These effects often produce symptoms in the affected region.

When searching for causes, researchers have generally postulated that three potent risk factors emerge as most significant:[9]

1. *Elevated cholesterol in the serum.* When the total cholesterol level in the blood is greater than 220 milligrams per deciliter, there is an increased risk of heart disease involved. Also, increased levels of blood fat (triglycerides) are associated with premature atherosclerosis.

2. *Hypertension.* The incidence of heart disease was upwards to five times higher for middle-age men with hypertension than for men with normal pressures. After one passes age fifty, hypertension is a more important factor than cholesterol level. The higher pressure is destructive to the arterial walls.

3. *Cigarette smoking.* Apparently the risk is greater in proportion to the amount of cigarettes smoked. When women smoke and also take oral contraceptives, there is an accumulation of atherosclerosis. There is also thought to be a relationship to carbon monoxide and reduced oxygen levels in smokers.

Other significant risk factors include:

Hyperglycemia: Elevated blood sugar.

Diabetes mellitus: This is associated with premature atherosclerosis worldwide.

Obesity: This association is stronger when the degree of obesity is greater than 30 percent above one's ideal weight.

Inactivity: Allows for increases in lipid levels in the blood, possibly due to decreased consumption of calories in energy expending activities.

Stress: Anxiety and emotional stresses are associated with precipitation of ischemic heart disease and even sudden death events.

6. Can atherosclerosis be halted or reversed?

This is the key question and probably one of the most significant in medicine today.[10]

Questions concerning this have been discussed since 1924. It was discovered that during World War I the incidence of heart attacks decreased. It was postulated that this occurrence was related to the low food supplies, particularly of cholesterol-rich foods. Among the post-World War II German population, the daily intake ranged in the 900 calories. Hospitals in three large centers reported not a single instance of death due to heart attack during this time.[11]

This has led researchers to suggest that maybe atherosclerosis can be halted or reversed. To review research on monkeys, dogs, pigs, pigeons, and rabbits, one finds that overfeeding these animals a diet rich in cholesterol leads to the development of patterns similar to those seen in humans known as atherosclerosis.[12] When the animals were given a low cholesterol diet, the arteries demonstrated nearly complete regression of these lesions.[13]

In human patients with cancer there has been a demonstration of regression of atherosclerosis.[14]

Intervention trials with a two-year vegetarian diet that contains less than 100 mg of cholesterol per day demonstrated, in some cases, a halting of progression of atherosclerosis. Even a few instances of reversal were seen.[15]

Halting the progression of coronary atherosclerosis may

be more reasonable and attainable than the complete regression of the atheromatous disruptions of the inner walls of the arteries.[16]

A *New York Times* article stated, "Lifestyle changes alone, without drugs or surgery, can halt or reverse atherosclerosis, a hardening of the arteries that can lead to heart attack, researchers reported yesterday."[17]

According to Dr. Alexander Leaf, director of the Cardiovascular Health Center at Massachusetts General Hospital, "This is going to shake up physicians' thinking."[18]

Studies done on fifty patients with coronary artery disease suggest that an intensive program of moderate exercise, fat restriction, smoking cessation, and stress management over a full year can achieve significant levels of cholesterol reduction and actual reversal of arterial blockage.[19]

Earlier studies suggesting that reducing cholesterol could slow or even reverse atherosclerosis had been reported in 1987 by Dr. David Blankenhorn, professor of medicine at the University of Southern California.[20]

Recent reviews of 1989 data from Framingham, Massachusetts, indicate that cardiovascular disease in general, coronary heart disease, and myocardial infarction all appear to have increased, even though the mortality has declined over the past thirty years.[21]

The incidence of heart attacks in Framingham over a thirty-year period among hypertensive patients who were receiving treatment has increased.[22] There was also an increase in heart attacks among those with normal blood pressure.

According to *U.S. News and World Report,* the same fatty diet that can lead to high blood cholesterol is also partly to blame for high blood pressure, colon cancer and other life-threatening conditions.[23]

We are winning the battle, but apparently losing the war. Perhaps it's time to consider a new tactic.

He who is slow in making a promise
is the most faithful
in the performance of it.[1]

13

The Key Ingredient: Follow-Up

You have learned new ways to deal with your hypertension. You have read in depth about the necessary factors for control. Your exercise needs have been addressed and relaxation techniques have also been taught.

Once you have completed the Plus Fifteen program and your blood pressure has been restored to normal, what then? Now you must focus on maintaining the ground you gained. How do you do it? Again, it comes down to the four areas of concentration:

1. Time and Priority
2. Order and Organization
3. Consistency
4. Commitment

On top of that we suggest the following plan for meeting with your doctor on a regular basis to help you maintain your newly adopted lifestyle:

1. Make an appointment to see your doctor approximately one month from the conclusion of Plus Fifteen.
2. See your doctor monthly for the first six months to check your blood pressure.
3. See your doctor every two months for the following six months.

4. Thereafter, see your doctor quarterly for follow-up on your blood pressure, cholesterol, urinalysis, and any other problem areas you might face.

5. At the conclusion of one year, consider redoing your Plus Fifteen program if possible.

6. After completing the program, evaluate which steps had the greatest benefit to you in restoring your blood pressure to normal. Incorporate these steps into your daily routine.

7. Remember, it takes time and practice. Keep the faith!

The lost coin, in the Savior's parable,
though lying in the dirt and rubbish,
was a piece of silver still.[1]

14

Why
It Works

One day I stopped at the home of a long-time friend just north of New York City to say hello. We chatted for a while and enjoyed a few laughs about old times. In the course of our visit, I noticed an odd-looking contraption in one corner of the room that appeared unusually weird and decidedly unfamiliar. I inquired, "What on earth is that?"

He smiled and began to unravel the mystery of this new invention. He had been introduced to a young engineer who by nearly anyone's evaluation would be classed as a near genius. This engineer had been captivated with the study of energy and its varied sources, uses and supply. At one time he was honored with the "Inventor of the Year" award of western New York, following submission of one of his patented developments. But as yet, no one had really discovered him.

The contraption in the corner of the room was only one of nearly fifty inventions he had developed over a course of years. This curious machine was a special generator capable of producing an alternate fuel to power automobiles and other machines. The inventor had demonstrated his invention to my friend by driving his car through the streets and thru-ways of New York for more than four continuous hours without any gasoline in the tank.

Later, I met the inventor and invited him to my home. He ran our gas clothes dryer, heated our home, and operated our lawn tractor without using any of the standard fuels. I was absolutely amazed at the potential for his surprising invention. It was not difficult to make me a believer when he fully demonstrated the potential of his contraption.

One big question in my mind remained: Why does it work? What's the secret?

As we reflect on Plus Fifteen, we often ask this same question — why does it work?

The Additive Effect

Often we hear reports of how something lowers blood pressure. Take, for example, the concept of rest and relaxation. To a degree, we can demonstrate advantages of rest in blood pressure reduction, but we are quite aware that rest alone is not the answer.

Other factors such as exercise or diet also function to lower blood pressure levels toward normal, but fall short of completing the job of total restoration.

However, the effect of a *combination* of well-researched lifestyle factors clearly demonstrates the additive effect of the individual factors taken together. That's why Plus Fifteen works. It is a logical combination of lifestyle factors with those weighted strongest introduced first.

One physician jokingly asked me, "What kind of hocus pocus is this?" Many have allowed physiological principles to fade into the background of medicine. But the additive effect of physiological principles is what makes Plus Fifteen work. It's a composite approach, a return to a simpler life and practice.

The Experience of Other Researchers

Many years ago I visited throughout Africa and discovered that the array of physical ailments was dramatically different from my North American experience and background. Heart attacks were rare to non-existent; strokes and cancer were not as common. The incidence of high blood pressure was significantly less than my Western frame of reference had taught me to expect.

I was pleased when I heard of the work of Dr. Nathan Pritikin in Santa Barbara, California, and made every effort to visit him and to interview his patients in the program. Convinced he was on the right course, I began considering the implications for high blood pressure control by physiological means.

Several excursions to the Cooper Clinic in Dallas, Texas, and various visits with Dr. Kenneth Cooper reinforced the concept and value of a lifestyle approach to high blood pressure control. I realized that an emphasis in this country on lifestyle could produce favorable results on blood pressure control without drugs.

In 1975, I began to formulate a protocol for the treatment of high blood pressure without drugs. I went to the dean of the school of medicine where I was training and presented my program, asking him to critique the concept.

I later presented the concept to Dr. Rochella at the National Institute of Health in Bethesda. We were at the time attempting to develop a center for the lifestyle focus in Nashville, Tennessee, as a treatment approach to high blood pressure control.

I was pleased then to see the book by Dr. Cleaves Bennett on blood pressure control without drugs and the founding of the Bircher-Benner Clinic in Zurich, Switzerland. Books by such authors as Dr. Zugibe, Dr. Whitaker, and Dr. Rowan confirmed the value of a lifestyle approach to blood pressure control. It made good sense.

The Ancient Scriptures

It's amazing to think that the health concepts encapsulated thousands of years ago in the Holy Scriptures form the basis for approaching high blood pressure control by lifestyle.

Who ever would have thought that a potent weapon against our greatest killer disease today — atherosclerosis — was so plainly stated in Holy Scripture over three thousand years ago for all to heed:

It shall be a perpetual statute for your generations

throughout all your dwellings that ye eat neither fat nor blood (Leviticus 3:17).

The combined concepts of Plus Fifteen can largely be found inculcated in the Holy Scriptures if one takes the time to look for them. We can have confidence in the outcomes of this program, when it is carefully followed. Its principles are as old as time.

If thou wilt diligently hearken to the voice of thy God, and wilt do that which is right in his sight, and wilt give ear to his commandments, and keep all his statutes, I will put none of these diseases upon thee (Exodus 15:26).

Pure air, sunlight, abstemiousness, rest,
exercise, proper diet, the use of water, trust in
the divine power — these are the true remedies.[1]

15

The Proof
of the Pudding

Rarely will a new program be met with much enthusiasm if such a program causes pain. One experiences pain when he is told he must give up a cherished habit.

Some bad habits are inculcated in the concepts of fun and pleasure, thus becoming even more difficult to give up. Food is deeply ingrained in the psyche. We must remember that food is not just food. Eppright says it so well: "Food is the crossroads of emotions, of religion, of culture, and beliefs."

Yet, we are encouraged by those who have the courage to attempt to do something good for themselves in healthful practices. We'd like to introduce some of our candidates who have completed the Plus Fifteen program. An old adage says: "The proof of the pudding is in the tasting." The proof of Plus Fifteen is found in its graduates, who have graciously given me permission to share their comments. I've chosen to refer to them by their initials only for the sake of privacy.

"The Plus Fifteen program has been a total success for me. I not only had a decrease in blood pressure from 180/112 to 124/80, but I also lost ten pounds in fifteen days and learned to control the stress factors in my life that had gotten out of hand."

S. C.

"This class has meant more to me than anyone on earth will know. I have learned more about what food means to your body as far as life and health are concerned.

"My plans are to stay on this diet for the rest of my life."

A. T.

"I have been very impressed with the goals and philosophy of the Plus Fifteen program. It has alerted me to the importance of daily blood pressure monitoring.

"I have benefited from this fifteen-day period by increasing my water intake to ten glasses per day. The most spectacular change in lifestyle has been the elimination of salt in cooking and at the table and a more conscientious effort to avoid high-sodium foods. I did experience a six-pound weight loss during this period."

R. H.

"The Plus Fifteen program has been a delightful, enlightening experience. I will continue to try to follow the information I have gained and I am very proud of my blood pressure. This information and experience will be shared with my friends."

Q. P. B.

"Plus Fifteen is one the best things that has ever happened to me because I've often tried to lose weight but was not going about it in the right way.

"Plus Fifteen has helped and informed me physically as well as spiritually on how to lose weight and take care of my blood pressure. When I joined Plus Fifteen, my blood pressure was above normal, but now I get a normal reading and I'm on my way to losing more weight.

"Thank you to you and the staff. Most of all, I thank God for bringing you back to America to help us."

M. C.

"This is the second time I took Plus Fifteen. I began with readings at 180/130 mm Hg some eighteen months ago. Repeating Plus Fifteen was very worthwhile. [His most recent readings were 120/90 mm Hg.]

"A total life readjustment is needed so it takes some repeated interaction with all the aspects of life that contribute to giving us high blood pressure to get the full benefits of Plus Fifteen.

"I had never previously dieted. Getting off the salt habit involved six months, for my system was still accustomed to too many years of too much salt. But after only a month, food began tasting better."

R. A.

"I appreciate the menus and the emphasis on the exercise program. I am looking forward to the follow-up program. I feel I have been enlightened and have had some success, but now I am going to reach my goal with my weight and my blood pressure."

L. P.

"Thank you for inviting me to this program. The idea of cutting out sugar and salt and lowering fats is a marvelous plan! Just to see the weight drop off so easily by following this plan has been a great encouragement to me! I'm very appreciative. I need so much to lose another 75 pounds so I want to continue putting this diet into action as much as possible. My starting blood pressure was 142/100 on February 28 and is now 122/88 on March 12. My weight went from 235 to 225 pounds."

D. M. K.

"Plus Fifteen is an excellent program. Before starting this program, my weight was 195 pounds and my blood pressure was 178/120 mm Hg and my EKG showed PVCs [extra beats]. I was not on any medication. With exercise, hydrotherapy, diet and breathing techniques, my whole lifestyle changed. My weight is now 185 pounds and my blood pressure is 100/70 mm Hg."

D. G.

"Plus Fifteen reminded me of the National Association of Recreation's slogan — 'Life: Be In It.' Being involved with Plus Fifteen has reconfirmed how great one can feel through proper diet and sound exercise. I've gained an awareness about stress factors, and I realize the importance of relaxation.

"I feel terrific! I truly have gained a new lease on life."

M. P.

"Plus Fifteen has started me on the road of discovery and recovery. This program has shown me the benefits of following the Plus Fifteen steps, not just for fifteen days, but for the duration of my life. Since the onset of this program, my overall feelings are better, my heart no longer pounds, my blood pressure has dropped and my weight loss is ten pounds. I also lost inches. Thank you, Dr. and Mrs. DeShay."

C. H.

"I want to thank Dr. Samuel DeShay for Plus Fifteen. I have learned a lot from it. I have been telling everyone how I lost weight and how my blood pressure came way down by following your simple diet. I really appreciate this program."

W. C.

"My mother experienced a stroke recently which caused me to become quite concerned about my own chances of this happening. I entered this program to learn what I could do to lower my blood pressure without the use of any medication. As a result I received far more than I entered the program for. It would take more than this one paragraph to describe in detail all that I learned in just two weeks. In short, the results from walking, relaxing, and eating the suggested foods were normalization of blood pressure for both my mother and me, and the loss of seven pounds and a calmer nature for me. But the most treasured experience from this program was not the results of the blood pressure or the seven pounds weight loss, but the knowledge of how to change from the wrong way of living in this physical life to the way God intended for man to live."

C. P. W.

"Plus Fifteen is the best thing that's happened to me. I have learned how to relax. I didn't know I could eat without salt and have the food taste good. I have learned a lot more about the body functions. I have reached the point where, if I don't have my eight glasses of water and my daily exercise, I feel as if I've missed out on something.

"I have followed my program to the best of my ability. My blood pressure has come down. I have lost eight pounds, and I feel good about myself. I have more energy. I have no intention of having high blood pressure anymore. You gave me the secret and I intend to follow it."

H. B.

"When I first came to Dr. DeShay, he suggested I come to his Plus Fifteen class. I was a hyper and impatient person which did not help my blood pressure at all. I am grateful to say, after completing the course, I have learned to condition myself and am now a calmer and relaxed person.

"This course is an excellent tool and I have learned so much that I, in turn, have passed it on to members of my family. For many years I had to take medicine every day for my blood pressure. Now I'm taking medication every other day. I have learned to prepare tasty, filling meals and have learned to walk two miles or more each day and enjoy it. The course has helped me to have better health, control my blood pressure and lengthen my life span. Thank you, Dr. and Mrs. DeShay."

U. S.

"I started the Plus Fifteen class on February 28, 1988. When I first started, the diet was very hard for me because it consisted of no salt. I was very weak the first several days, but my body became adjusted the second week.

"Relaxation, spiritual values, exercise, hydrotherapy, and staying happy are just some of the recommendations given for the prevention of high blood pressure. They are all very rewarding.

"I was taking Dyazide daily when I started the class. After two weeks, I was taken off the medication. I lost eight pounds and my blood pressure is normal. I recommend Plus Fifteen to anyone suffering from high blood pressure."

L. V. J.

"Plus Fifteen was greatly beneficial to me physically and psychologically. For many years I have been very overweight with higher than normal blood pressure. I have begun many diet programs to reduce my weight and blood pressure but did not stay on them. I found the Plus Fifteen program more to my liking than any I have previously tried. It is easier to follow, and more geared to my lifestyle and eating habits. The large amount of fresh and dried fruits satisfied my persistent craving for sweets.

"Psychologically, my self-esteem has been significantly increased because of successfully lowering my blood pressure on the Plus Fifteen program from 182/110 to 142/90 mm Hg. It is the impetus I needed and I pledge to adopt it as my continuing lifestyle to lose the necessary amount of weight and keep my blood pressure within the normal range."

T. L. A.

"Plus Fifteen has been a direct asset to my life. The diet has caused me to feel better and experience a new and delightful eating habit. My weight loss has been nine pounds and my blood pressure is normal."

A. H.

"I enjoyed the Plus Fifteen program. Even though I didn't lose any weight, I did get my blood pressure down below normal. I never thought I could enjoy eating salt-free foods, but the menus were mouth watering. It feels good being in the best of health."

M. M.

"I found Plus Fifteen to be very educational and helpful and I recommend it to anyone who is seriously desirous of lowering their blood pressure and losing weight. My pressure ended up lower than the normal range. It had been above normal for the past ten years."

E. A.

"The Lord is so good. This is the first time I've been able to lose any weight. Plus Fifteen has really changed my eating habits. Plus Fifteen has done so much for me. My pressure is down, and I lost nine pounds in the fifteen days. I think that is marvelous. Thank God for the research of Dr. DeShay and the concern of Mrs. DeShay."

C. R. C.

"The program has helped my blood pressure to reduce without medication and I do not have those headaches any more. I feel better because I haven't had the intake of sodium, sugar and fats. I also am happy to know about the use of olive oil."

I. M. S.

"Even though most of the information presented was not new to me, it was very beneficial to have this refresher course on healthful lifestyle. Ten pounds were lost during this program and I feel better for it.

"Thanks for the impetus to get back on track."

K. H. B.

"The program was of great benefit to me, not only in

terms of the physical, but more importantly in the growth of self-discipline since the program demanded conformity to a prescribed diet and regular exercise.

"I was able to effect the desired change in my diet but failed in doing the required amount of walking. This is an area in which I must concentrate in bringing about improvement. I lost seven pounds during the fifteen day period. I would say that the lesson I have learned is that I have to accept a significant degree of responsibility for lowering my blood pressure."

G. F.

Epilogue

Life is but a vapor, so quickly lost forever. As one poet puts it:

Life! We've been long together,
  Through pleasant and through cloudy weather;

'Tis hard to part when friends are dear—
  Perhaps 'twill cost a sigh, a tear;

Life, I know not what thou art,
  But know that thou and I must part.[1]

No matter the circumstance, death is an unwelcome intruder. If only life could be extended, what things we would change.

Health is one of those things we can do something about. One can take active steps toward achieving life enhancement and enrichment, a longer life.

Staggering health issues, those whose numbers of cases almost exceed imagination, face us today. Health costs to treat widespread chronic diseases are skyrocketing. The origins and course of their development are deeply rooted in our society and its lifestyle. Such mammoth problems as hypertension, obesity, heart disease, and elevated cholesterol seem to defy solution.

Some think the only way to handle these health problems is to administer another pill. Powerful self-interest groups fight to maintain the status quo if a certain measure of control might bring profit shifts or losses.

Thought leaders proclaim that we should trouble people's

lifestyles as little as possible. But the root of the problem *is* our lifestyle.

Leaving solutions to the experts has helped many to enjoy a more symptom-free life. However, the number of sufferers is growing daily. At the root of the problem is the dependence on someone else to make personal decisions for us even in matters of health and longevity. The question is Who has authority over my body? Who has more interest in it that I do? Shouldn't thinking people take more responsibility for their health and their future?

Responsibility rests upon a substantial knowledge base. Plus Fifteen addresses this concept for persons suffering from hypertension.

The very best advice on high blood pressure control is to prevent it. As Solomon states, "A prudent man foreseeth the evil, and hideth himself" (Proverbs 27:12). When you are lost, the answer is often to retrace your steps to discover how you arrived where you are, how you strayed from the path. Too often we reach for solutions which overlook how we came to our present state. Solutions often act as Band-Aids on much larger problems that demand larger answers.

Lifestyle Success Stories

For nearly a century, the Bircher-Benner clinic of Zurich, Switzerland, has treated high blood pressure, emphasizing dietary alteration, physical fitness, and other natural therapies. Patients on their program normalize their blood pressure in fifteen to thirty days.[2]

In an appropriate environment, patients have a greater chance of recovery and more time to devote to causation and the steps to recovery. In his Longevity Research Institute, Nathan Pritikin demonstrated the response of patients to alteration in lifestyle and restoration of high blood pressure.

More recently, Dr. Julian Whitaker of the National Heart and Diabetes Treatment Institute in Huntington Beach, California, in his book, *Reversing Heart Disease,* cited a case appropriate for this time:

Frank had a problem. He was a fifty-four-year-old airline

pilot, and was sure to lose his license. Commercial pilots may not have high blood pressure or be on medication for it and continue to fly. Frank checked into the Institute three weeks before his Federal Aeronautic Administration (FAA) physical examination with a blood pressure of 225/115. He had to get it down fast without medication, so we altered his diet even more radically than we usually do. Frank checked out of the Institute in twelve days with a blood pressure of 130/84, on no medication. One week later he passed his FAA physical with a blood pressure of 140/82. Almost three years later Frank is still flying, and he has a blood pressure of 120/75 with no medication.[3]

The Weimar Institute near Sacramento, California, has had remarkable results in restoring normality to patients with high blood pressure. The Hartland Institute in Rapidan, Virginia, has achieved impressive success as well.

One in five Americans is a potential candidate for taking antihypertensive medication.[4] There must be a better way to treat the disease. That better way might just be Plus Fifteen.

I like the way Louisa Fletcher put it in her poem, "The Land of Beginning Again":

> I wish that there were some wonderful place
> Called the Land of Beginning Again
> Where all our mistakes and all our heartaches
> And all of our poor selfish grief
> Could be dropped like a shabby old coat at the door
> And never be put on again.
>
> We would find all the things we intended to do
> But forgot and remembered too late
> Little praises unspoken, little promises broken
> And all of the thousand and one
> Little duties neglected that might have perfected
> The day for one less fortunate.
>
> For what had been hardest we'd know had been best,
> And what had seemed loss would be gain;
> For there isn't a sting that will not take wing
> When we faced it and laughed it away;
> And I think that the laughter is most what we're after
> In the Land of Beginning Again.[5]

The Plus Fifteen Menu

NOTE: Recipes for menu items marked by an asterik (*) appear at the end of this appendix.

DAY ONE

Breakfast
1 grapefruit

2 slices whole wheat toast

1 T date preserves*

1 C water

Lunch
1 C cooked brown rice*

1/2 C tomato sauce*

1 C tossed salad with fresh radishes, cucumber

1 T salad dressing*

Dinner
1 apple

1 orange

1 banana

1/8 C (2 T) raisins

Day Two

Breakfast
1 sliced orange

1 C cooked oatmeal

2 chopped dates

1 C skim milk

Lunch

1/2 C cooked noodles

2 C raw vegetable salad:
1 C lettuce
1/2 C sliced cucumber
3 radishes
1/2 C raw spinach

2 T salad dressing*

2 slices toast

1 C water

Dinner

1/2 cantaloupe

1/2 C applesauce

1/2 C strawberries

1 whole wheat/bran muffin*

Day Three

Breakfast

1 C whole grain cereal

1 C non-fat dry skim milk

1 medium banana

1/2 C orange juice

1 C water

Lunch

1 C cooked brown rice*

1/2 C tomato sauce*

1 C carrot/raisin salad*

1 C water

Dinner

1 C fruit cocktail in natural juice

2 slices whole wheat toast

1 T applebutter (natural)

1 C water

Day Four

Breakfast

15 grapes

2 slices whole wheat toast

2 T natural peanut butter (no salt or sugar added)
1/2 C applesauce (natural)
3/4 C Postum (cereal drink)
1 C skim milk

Lunch
1 C kidney beans*
1/2 C brown rice*
1 C salad (lettuce, tomato, cucumber)
1 T salad dressing*
1 C water

Dinner
1 1/2 C fresh fruit salad*
1 bagel or 2 slices whole grain bread
1 C water

Day Five

Breakfast
1/4 C crushed pineapple (natural juice)
2 whole grain waffles (low sodium)
1/2 C vanilla yogurt
1/8 C raisins
1 C water

Lunch
1 C garbanzo spread*
1 whole wheat pita bread
1/2 C tomatoes/cucumbers
1 large raw carrot
1 C water

Dinner
1 apple, diced
1 banana, sliced
1/2 C sliced peaches
6 prunes
1 bran muffin*
1 C water

Day Six

Breakfast
1 medium banana
3/4 C granola*

1 C skim milk
1/2 C orange juice

Lunch
1 Dinner Cut cacciatore*
1 C cabbage shredded
2 T salad dressing*
1 white potato (baked)

Dinner
3 C popcorn
1 pear
1 C iced tea

Day Seven

Breakfast
1 C grapefruit juice
3/4 C scrambled tofu*
2 slices whole wheat or rye bread
1/2 C applesauce
1 C water

Lunch
2 Linketts with 1/4 C tomato sauce*
1 medium baked potato, sweet or white
1 C cooked greens (kale, collards, spinach)*
1 whole wheat roll
1 C water

Dinner
3/4 C garbanzo salad
1 whole wheat pita bread
1/2 C lettuce and tomato
1 C water

Day Eight

Breakfast
15 grapes
2 slices whole wheat bread
1 T homemade preserves* or 1/2 C applesauce
1/2 C skim milk
1 C water

Lunch
1 C cooked brown rice*
1 C lentil soup*
1 C sliced tomato, cucumber, radishes, lettuce, spinach
1 T salad dressing*

Dinner
1 C fresh fruit salad*
1 whole grain/bran muffin*
1 C water

Day Nine

Breakfast
1 C cream of wheat (multigrain cereal)
1 C skim milk
4 dates
1 slice whole wheat toast
1 orange

Lunch
Pasta salad:
1 C whole wheat noodles
1 tomato diced
1/2 carrot shredded
3 radishes sliced
1/2 C cucumber
1/4 C kidney beans*
2 T bean sprouts
2 T salad dressing*
1 roll (whole grain roll or slice of bread)

Dinner
1 C canned apricot or peach halves in natural juice
1 pear
1 whole wheat bagel
1 T homemade preserves* or 2 dates

Day Ten

Breakfast
2 slices rye bread
1 Linkett*
1 C applesauce
1 C skim milk

Lunch
1 C baked beans*
1 C brown rice*
1/2 C cooked spinach*
1 C tossed salad
1 T salad dressing*

Dinner
1 1/2 C fruit salad:
1/2 C strawberries
1/2 C watermelon
1 medium banana
1/2 C fruit cocktail (or use peaches from day before)
1 whole wheat roll or 2 slices whole wheat bread
1/2 T peanut butter

Day Eleven

Breakfast
1 C grapefruit juice
1 C scrambled tofu*
2 slices rye bread
1/2 C applesauce
1 C water

Lunch
1 C kidney beans*
1 C brown rice*
1 C carrot raisin salad*
1 pear
1 C water

Dinner
1 Vegeburger pattie* on 1 whole wheat bun
1/2 C lettuce
1/2 tomato, sliced
1 apple

Day Twelve

Breakfast
1 medium orange
3/4 C granola*
1 C skim milk
1 medium banana
1 C water

Lunch
3/4 C cooked black eyed peas*
1 baked sweet potato
1 C collard greens*
1 corn muffin*
1/2 C tomato/cucumber
1 C water

Dinner
1 C fresh fruit salad*
1 slice whole wheat toast
1 T peanut butter (natural)

Day Thirteen

Breakfast
1 C whole grain cereal
1 C non-fat milk
1/2 C grapes
1/2 C orange juice

Lunch
1 C lentil soup*
2 corn muffins*
1 C coleslaw/carrot (buy the grated cabbage/carrot
and mix with 1 T salad dressing*)
1 medium baked potato

Dinner
1 Linkett* on whole wheat bun
1/2 C lettuce and tomatoes
1 peach

Day Fourteen

Breakfast
1 grapefruit
2 slices whole wheat toast
1 T date preserves*
1 C water

Lunch
1 C cooked brown rice*
1/2 C tomato sauce*
1 C tossed salad with fresh mushrooms and radishes
1 T salad dressing*

Dinner
1 apple
1 orange
1 banana
1 corn muffin*

Day Fifteen

Breakfast
1 sliced orange
1 C cooked oatmeal
2 chopped dates
1 C skim milk

Lunch
1/2 C cooked noodles
2 C raw vegetable salad:
1 C lettuce
1/2 C sliced cucumber
3 radishes
1/2 C raw spinach
2 T salad dressing*
2 slices toast
1 C water

Dinner
1/2 C cantaloupe
1/2 C applesauce
1/2 C strawberries
1 whole wheat/bran muffin*

Recipes

Brown Rice

Boil 2 C water. Add 1 C brown rice and cover. Cook slowly for 20 to 30 minutes on medium heat until soft. Yields 2 to 2 1/2 C. Rice may be used as a vegetable, cereal or mixed equally with fruit as a dessert.

Date Preserves

1 C chopped dates   1/2 C crushed pineapple in
                           natural juice

Blend ingredients together. Yields 16 to 20 tablespoons.

Salad Dressing

1/4 C olive oil
1 t herb seasoning:
  1/4 t garlic powder
  1/4 t grated onion
  1/4 t parsley
  1/4 t basil

1/4 C lemon juice
2 T honey (optional)

Mix seasonings in lemon juice. Add to oil and honey. Shake well. Store in refrigerator.

Lentil Soup

2 C lentils (dry)
2 quarts hot water
1 large onion, chopped
2 stalks chopped celery
2 bay leaves

1/2 can (6 oz.) tomato paste (no sodium)
1 carrot, finely chopped
1/4 C parsley, chopped
2 t garlic powder
1 t Mrs. Dash's seasoning (optional)

Cook lentils in hot water with bay leaf until done (approximately 20 minutes). Add other ingredients, simmering for 30 to 45 minutes. Store unused portion in refrigerator. Yields 6 to 8 servings.

Tomato Sauce

1 12 oz. can tomato paste
  (no sodium)
1 T seasonings (mix as desired): thyme, sage, basil, rosemary, chili
  powder, paprika, marjoram
1/4 C honey (if allowed on your diet)

18 oz. water (add more if desired)

Mix all ingredients well. Cook over low heat until seasonings are well blended (about 30 to 45 minutes). Store in your refrigerator and use when tomato sauce is needed. Yields 16 to 20 oz.

Greens (kale, collard or spinach)

2 pounds of greens
1 chopped green pepper
1/4 C water (do not add water to spinach)
1 T Mrs. Dash's seasoning (optional)

2 T olive oil
1 C chopped or sliced onions

Wash and chop greens. Set aside. Sauté onions, green peppers and oil together in large sauce pan. Add chopped greens and 1/4 C water. Cover and cook slowly, stirring frequently until done, usually 20 to 30 minutes. Yields 4 to 6 servings.

Scrambled Tofu

1 pound tofu
1/2 C chopped onions
1 t tumeric

2 T olive oil
1/2 C chopped green peppers
1 t garlic powder

1 t chicken seasoning   1/8 t salt
1 t Mrs. Dash's seasoning (optional)

Rinse and drain tofu. Braise onions and green peppers in olive oil for 2 to 5 minutes. Add tofu and seasonings. Simmer an additional 10 to 15 minutes. Stir often to keep from sticking and serve warm. Add 1/8 t salt last, just before serving. Yields 4 servings.

Vegeburgers

1 C dry vegetable protein granules   1 C hot water
3 T chopped onions   3 T chopped green peppers
2 T flour   1/4 C oatmeal
1 T sage   1/4 t each — cumin, basil, chili pepper
2 T olive oil

Soak vegetable protein granules in hot water for 15 minutes. Add other ingredients and mix well. Allow to sit 15 to 20 minutes. Form into patties. Brown in 2 T olive oil. Yields 6 to 8 patties.

Beans

To cook dry beans, soak 1 C beans in 1 quart of water overnight. When ready to cook, boil 1 quart water and add soaked beans. Reduce heat. Cook until tender (usually 1 to 2 hours, depending on beans). Season by adding 1/4 C chopped onions, 1/4 C chopped green peppers, 1 T Mrs. Dash's seasoning, 2 T olive oil. Simmer for 15 minutes. Yields 4 to 6 servings.

Carrot, Pineapple and Raisin Salad

1 C grated carrots   1/2 C diced pineapple in own juice
1/2 C raisins   1 t mayonaise (low fat)
1 T chopped walnuts

Drain pineapple. Mix all ingredients together. Yields 1 serving.

Fresh Fruit Salad

2 oranges, cut in small pieces   2 apples, diced
1 large banana, diced or sliced   1/4 C raisins
2 pears, diced   1/2 C plain yogurt (optional)
1/4 C walnuts, chopped

Mix all ingredients well. Yields 4 servings.

Garbanzo Spread or Dip

1 can (15 oz.) garbanzos   2 T low-fat mayonnaise/salad dressing
1 T chopped onions   1 clove garlic, minced
1 t parsley flakes   1/4 t basil
1/8 t salt   1/4 t tumeric

Wash garbanzos and mash well with fork. Mix all ingredients together. Yields 1 to 1 1/2 C. For Dip add: 1/4 C water, 1/4 C lemon juice and mix in blender. Yields 2 C.

Granola

6 C oats (not quick cooking)	1/2 C walnuts
1/4 C shredded coconut	1 1/2 C liquid consisting of:
	1/4 C oil
	1/4 C honey
	1 C water
	1 t vanilla

Mix dry ingredients together. Pour liquid over dry ingredients, stirring with a fork until moist. Stir well to avoid lumps. Place on a cookie sheet. Bake 325° for one hour. Stir every 10 to 15 minutes. Store in sealed plastic or glass container. Yields 1 1/2 quarts.

Bran Muffins

2 C flour, unbleached or whole wheat	1 C wheat bran
2 T low-sodium baking power	1/2 C oat bran
1/4 C sugar	1 3/4 C water or skim milk (soy milk is also good)
1/4 C olive oil	1 C raisins (optional)

Oil muffin tins and set aside. Mix dry ingredients on low speed of mixer or by hand. Gradually add oil and water (milk) until moist. Add raisins if desired. Do not overbeat. Place in muffin tins. Bake at 350° for 30 to 40 minutes, until done. Yields 12 muffins.

The dry mixture may be made ahead and stored in a tightly sealed jar or container. Add the liquid just before cooking.

Dinner Cut Cacciatore

Note: Linketts and Dinner Cuts are protein analogues (vegetable proteins) that may be purchased at health stores.

4 Dinner Cuts	1 T olive oil
1/4 C sliced onions	1 C whole tomatoes
1/4 C chopped green peppers	1 C tomato sauce*
1 t basil	1/4 C apple juice with 2 T lemon juice
1 t oregano	

Braise onions and green peppers in olive oil. Add Dinner Cuts, tomatoes and tomato sauce. Simmer 15 to 20 minutes. Add apple/lemon juice. Heat 5 more minutes and serve hot. Yields 4 servings.

Baked Beans

1 lb. white navy beans
1/2 C chopped green peppers
1 T Mrs. Dash's seasoning
1/2 C water
1/4 C molasses

1 bay leaf
1/2 C chopped onions
3 oz. tomato paste (no sodium)
2 T olive oil

Cook beans with bay leaf until soft, but not mushy. In large skillet, sauté onions and peppers in oil. Add 4 to 5 C cooked beans, seasonings, tomato paste, water and molasses. Place in baking dish and bake at 350° for 30 to 45 minutes until bubbly. Yields 6 to 8 servings.

Corn Muffins

1 1/2 C unbleached flour
1/4 C sugar
1/3 C olive oil

1 C corn meal
2 T low-sodium baking powder
1 1/4 C skim milk or water

Oil 12 muffin tins. Sift dry ingredients together. Mix oil and water and add to dry mixture until moist. Do not overmix. Place in muffin tins. Bake at 350° for 30 to 45 minutes until done. Yields 12 muffins.

Permitted Foods

Below are listed food items to help you plan future meals. Recipes for items marked ** are available from Plus Fifteen, 7610 Carroll Ave., Suite 320, Takoma Park, MD 20912.

Fruit Group

One serving provides approximately 20 grams of carbohydrate, a trace of protein and fat, and 80 calories.

Apple, 1 medium
Applesauce, 1/2 C
Apple, baked**
Banana, 1 small
Banana/Pineapple Ice Cream,**
    1/2 C
Blackberries, fresh, 1 C
Blueberries, fresh, 1 C
Boysenberries, fresh, 1 C
Cantaloupe, 1/2 medium melon
Cherries, fresh, 18 large
Dates, 3 medium
Figs, 2 large
Grapefruit, 1 medium
Grapes, fresh, 3/4 C
Guava, 1 medium
Lemons, 2 medium

Mango, 1/2 medium
Nectarines, 2 medium
Orange, 1 medium
Papaya, 2/3 medium
Peaches, 2 medium, 1 C sliced
Pear, 1 small
Persimmon, 1 medium
Pineapple, fresh, 1 C
Plums, 2 medium
Prunes, 3 medium
Pomegranate, 1 large
Raisins, 2 1/2 t
Raspberries, fresh, 1 C
Sauce for fruit toast,** 1/2 C
Strawberries, fresh, 1 1/3 C
Tangerines, 2 large
Watermelon slice, 6" diameter, 3/4" thick

Grain and Cereal Group

One serving provides approximately 3 gm of protein, 18 gm of complex carbohydrates, and 100 calories.

Bread, whole grain, 1 1/2 slices
Breakfast cereals, prepared
    All Bran, 1/2 C
    40% Bran Flakes, 3/4 C
    Grapenuts, 1/4 C
    Shredded Wheat,
      1 1/4 biscuits
    Wheat Chex, 1/2 C
    Wheaties, 1 C
    Cooked cereals,
      whole-grain, 3/4 C
Corn, cooked, 3/4 C
Corn on the cob, 1 medium ear

Cornmeal, whole-grain, 1/4 C
Oatmeal, dry, 1/4 C
Oatmeal, cooked, 3/4 C
Pancake, whole-grain,** 1
Rice, brown, cooked, 3/4 C
Roll, 1 average
Rye Crisp, 4 to 5 small wafers
Rye flour, 1/3 C
Soy-oat waffle, 4" x 4", 1
Tortilla, corn, 6" diameter, 1 1/2
Wheat, cracked, cooked, 2/3 C
Wheat flour, whole-grain, 1/4 C
Wheat germ, 3 T

Fat Group

One serving provides approximately 5 gm of fat and 45 calories.

Mayonnaise, imitation, 1 1/2 t
Vegetable oil, 1 t

Margarine, 1 t
Dry salad dressings (mixed with
         buttermilk and mayonnaise)

Not Permitted

Butter
Lard and shortening
Hard stick margarine

Commercial salad dressings
Gravy (made from fat)

Note: Measure all fats very carefully. *Instruction on which margarine to buy:* Check list of ingredients and the *first* item listed should be *liquid oil* (either soy, corn or safflower), *not* partially hardened or hydrogenated. Check both tub and stick margarine before buying.

Food Choices for Fat

Dairy Products

Skim milk, 1 C (0.2 gm)
Low fat milk, 1 C (4.9 gm)
Uncreamed cottage cheese,
    1/2 C (0.2 gm)
Creamed CC, 1/2 C (4.4 gm)
American cheese, 1/2 slice (4.3 gm)
Yogurt (skim), 1 C (4.2 gm)
Avocado, 1/6 whole (6.1 gm)

"Natural" Fats

Almonds, 10 (5.4 gm)
Brazil Nuts, 3 (9.1 gm)
Cashews, 9 (6.5 gm)
Pecans, 10 (6.4 gm)
Peanuts, 10 (8.8 gm)
Walnuts, Eng., 10 (7.3 gm)
Olives, 5 large (4.0 gm)

Visible Fats

Oil, cooking, 1 t (4.5 gm)
Peanut butter, 1 T (8.1 gm)

Margarine
    Whipped, 1 t (2.6 gm)
    Regular soft, 1 t (3.8 gm)

Vegetable Group

One serving provides approximately 2 gm of protein, 8 gm of complex carbohydrates, a trace of polyunsaturated fats, and 40 calories.

Asparagus, 7-8 spears
Beans, green snap, 1 C, cooked
Beans, sprouts, 1 1/2 C
Beets, 2 beets, 2" diameter
Broccoli, 1 1/2 stalks or 1 C
Brussel sprouts, 7-8 medium
Cabbage, 1 1/2 C raw shredded,
   1 C cooked
Carrots, 1 large, 2 small,
   1 C cooked
Cauliflower, 1 C
Celery, use as desired
Chard, 1 C cooked
Collards, 1/2 C cooked
Cucumbers, use as desired
Egg Plant, 3 slices
Kale, 3/4 C cooked
Lettuce and other salad greens,
   use as desired
Mushrooms, 12-14 small, 6 large

Mustard greens, 3/4 C cooked
Onions, 1 small
Onions, green, 4 small,
   including tops
Parsnips, 1/2 small, or 1/3 C
Peas, green, 1/2 C
Peppers, green, use as desired
Potatoes, 1/2 small, 2/5 C cooked
Pumpkin, 1/2 C cooked
Radishes, use as desired
Rutabagas, 3 oz. raw, 1/2 C cooked
Spinach, 1 C cooked
Squash, summer, 1 C cooked
Squash, winter, 2/5 C cooked
Sweet potatoes, 1/3 small, 1/3 C cooked
Tomato, 1 medium
Tomato juice, 1 C
Turnip greens, 1 C cooked
Vegetable juice cocktail, 1 C
Yams, 1/3 C cooked

Milk Group

One serving provides approximately 9 gm protein, 12 grams of carbohydrate, and 90 calories.

Buttermilk (made from
   skim milk), 1 C
Skim milk (non-fat), 1 cup

Soy milk (non-fat), 1 C
Yogurt (made from skim milk), 1 C

Not Permitted
Whole milk
Cream
Non-dairy creamers
Cream substitutes

Protein-rich Group

One serving provides approximately 15 gm of protein, 40 gm of complex carbohydrates, 2.5 gm of polyunsaturated fats, and 240 calories.

Legumes, cooked**
Brown beans, 1 C
Chickpeas (garbanzos), 1 C
Cuban black beans, 1 C
Kidney beans, 1 C
Lentils, 1 C
Lima beans, 1 C

Savory Patties,** 2
Scrambled Tofu, 3/4 C
Shepherd's Stew,** 1 1/2 C
Spanish lentils,** 1 C
Split pea soup,** 1 1/3 C
Soy Patties Supreme,** 2
Supreme Loaf,** 1/2 C

Navy beans, 1 C
Pinto beans, 1 C
Soybeans, 2/3 C
Bean chowder,** 1 1/2 C
   (includes 1 vegetable serving)
Chili beans, 1 C
  Come-and-Get-It Soup,**
   1 1/2C (includes 1 vegetable
   serving)
Duchess Roast,** 1/2 C
Festive Loaf,** 1/2 C
Four-bean Salad,** 1 C
Grandma's Roast or Patties,**
  1/2 C
Minestrone Soup,** 1 1/2 C
   (includes 1 vegetable serving)
Pioneer Patties,** 2
Plantation Patties,** 2
Pronto Patties,** 2
Princess Patties,** 2

Vegeburgers,** 2
Vegetable Stew,** 1 1/2 C
   (includes 1 vegetable serving)
Viking Roast,** 1/2C
Vitaburgers**, 1 (1/3 C mix)

Other alternates:
Cottage cheese, low fat, 1/2 C
Egg white (1 contains only 6 calories
  and 6.5 gm of protein. Use in
  entree preparation and count as
  part of entree serving.)
Peanut butter, 3 T (omit 3 additional
  fat exchanges)
Tofu (soy cheese), 2/3 C
TVP (textured vegetable protein),
  dry, 2 oz. Use in entrees and
  stews, etc. Count as part of
  entree.
Eggbeaters, 1/2 C (Equivalent to 2
  2 eggs. Would not contain the
  the complex carbohydrate.)

1800-Calorie Sample Meal Plan
Maintenance Diet—Plus Fifteen

BREAKFAST

Fruits - 2
Protein-rich - 1
Cereal-Grain - 2
Milk - 1

LUNCH

Protein-rich - 1
Vegetables - 3
Cereal-Grain - 2
Milk - 1 (or save)

SUPPER

Vegetable - 1
Cereal-Grain - 2
Fruits - 2

Three fat servings may be used. Fats used in cooking must be counted.

Appendix B: Biblical Health Principles

TEXT	SUMMARY STATEMENT	PRINCIPLE TODAY	RESULT ON TODAY'S SOCIETY
Happiness Proverbs 17:22	A merry heart doth good like a medicine. A broken spirit drieth the bones.	Cultivate the positive emotions.	Reduces tension, promotes good will and pleasant surroundings.
Rest/Relaxation Matthew 6:31	Come ye apart and rest awhile.	Take a break from your activities periodically to rest and relax.	A useful method for lowering tensions, anxiety, and reducing blood pressure.
Spreading Infections Leviticus 15	Beware the running issue and contamination fomites.	Be careful not to spread infectious agents (from obviously infected persons).	Reduction in advance of an infectious disease process within a community
Circumcision Genesis 17	Circumcise the male foreskin.	Easier cleaning/less disease spread.	Decrease incidence of cancer of cervix and cancer of penis (worldwide).
Overeating Deuteronomy 21:20,21 Ecclesiastes 22:6,7	Temperance. Those who are undisciplined should be counseled.	Limits are needed on intemperate behavior.	Decrease obesity.
Conservation Deuteronomy 20:19,20 Deuteronomy 22:6,7	Do not destroy the trees. Do not destroy the birds.	Consider the value of trees and birds before destroying them.	Less soil erosion, less misuse of land and abuse of nature.
Trust/Faith Mark 4:40 Mark 5:34	Why are ye so fearful? How is it that ye have no faith?	Trust in God for your health.	Much unrest, anxiety, guilt, is due to lack of faith — potent causes of disease.

TEXT	SUMMARY STATEMENT	PRINCIPLE TODAY	RESULT ON TODAY'S SOCIETY
Education Deuteronomy 6:6,7	Children are to be taught diligently during daily common activities.	Incorporate health information to family into all activities.	Health behavior change.
Work Ethic Genesis 3:19	"In the sweat of thy face shalt thou eat bread."	Work (physical labor) is the appointed method for food gathering (farming).	Farmers live longer than any other occupational group.
Food Selection Genesis 1:29 Genesis 3:18	Fruits, nuts, and vegetables were man's original diet.	Plant diet for the world is the best, most nutritive value.	Longer life/ less disease; more calories per acre available.
Food Prohibition Leviticus 3:17	Thou shalt eat neither fat nor blood — a perpetual statute.	Animal fat is to be discarded from the diet.	Severely curtails atherosclerosis — leading killer in Western society.
Liquor Use Proverbs 20:1 Proverbs 23:31,32	Wine is a mocker. It biteth like a serpent and stingeth like an adder.	Beware of using wine. It is a destroyer.	Decrease crimes committed, health care costs; birth defects, drug abuse.
Disposal of Wastes Deuteronomy 23:10-14	Bury the excreta with a shovel.	Handle human wastes properly.	Enormous reduction in health problems in third world countries (75%) now suffering with infectious diseases as a result of the mishandling of wastes.

Would You Like to Know God Personally?

The following four principles will help you discover how to know God personally and experience the abundant life He promised.

1 GOD **LOVES** YOU AND CREATED YOU TO KNOW HIM PERSONALLY.

(References contained in these pages should be read in context from the Bible whenever possible.)

God's Love

"For God so loved the world, that He gave His only begotten Son, that whoever believes in Him should not perish, but have eternal life" (John 3:16).

God's Plan

"Now this is eternal life: that they may know you, the only true God, and Jesus Christ, whom you have sent" (John 17:3, NIV).

What prevents us from knowing God personally?

(A version of the Four Spiritual Laws, written by Bill Bright. Copyright 1965, 1988, Campus Crusade for Christ, Inc. All rights reserved.)

2 MAN IS **SINFUL** AND **SEPARATED** FROM GOD, SO WE CANNOT KNOW HIM PERSONALLY OR EXPERIENCE HIS LOVE.

Man Is Sinful

"For all have sinned and fall short of the glory of God" (Romans 3:23).

Man was created to have fellowship with God; but, because of his stubborn self-will, he chose to go his own independent way, and fellowship with God was broken. This self-will, characterized by an attitude of active rebellion or passive indifference, is evidence of what the Bible calls sin.

Man Is Separated

"For the wages of sin is death" (spiritual separation from God) (Romans 6:23).

This diagram illustrates that God is holy and man is sinful. A great gulf separates the two. The arrows illustrate that man is continually trying to reach God and establish a personal relationship with Him through his own efforts, such as a good life, philosophy or religion.

The third principle explains the only way to bridge this gulf . . .

3 JESUS CHRIST IS GOD'S **ONLY** PROVISION FOR MAN'S SIN. THROUGH HIM ALONE WE CAN KNOW GOD PERSONAL-LY AND EXPERIENCE HIS LOVE.

He Died in Our Place

"But God demonstrates His own love toward us, in that while we were yet sinners, Christ died for us" (Romans 5:8).

He Rose From the Dead

"Christ died for our sins . . . He was buried . . . He was raised on the third day, according to the Scriptures . . . He appeared to Peter, then to the twelve. After that He appeared to more than five hundred" (1 Corinthians 15:3-6).

He Is the Only Way to God

"Jesus said to him, 'I am the way, and the truth, and the life; no one comes to the Father, but through Me' " (John 14:6).

This diagram illustrates that God has bridged the gulf which separates us from Him by sending His Son, Jesus Christ, to die on the cross in our place to pay the penalty for our sins.

```
        GOD  J
         |   E
         |   S
         v   U
       MAN   S
```

It is not enough just to know these truths...

4 WE MUST INDIVIDUALLY **RECEIVE** JESUS CHRIST AS SAVIOR AND LORD; THEN WE CAN KNOW GOD PERSONALLY AND EXPERIENCE HIS LOVE.

We Must Receive Christ

"But as many as received Him, to them He gave the right to become children of God, even to those who believe in His name" (John 1:12).

We Receive Christ Through Faith

"For by grace you have been saved through faith; and that not of yourselves, it is the gift of God; not as a result of works, that no one should boast" (Ephesians 2:8,9).

When We Receive Christ, We Experience a New Birth. (Read John 3:1-8.)

We Receive Christ by Personal Invitation

(Christ is speaking): "Behold, I stand at the door and knock; if anyone hears My voice and opens the door, I will come in to him" (Revelation 3:20).

Receiving Christ involves turning to God from self (repentance) and trusting Christ to come into our lives to forgive our sins and to make us the kind of people He wants us to be. Just to agree intellectually that Jesus Christ is the Son of God and that He died on the cross for our sins is not enough. Nor is it enough to have an emotional experience. We receive Jesus Christ by faith, as an act of the will.

These two circles represent two kinds of lives:

SELF-DIRECTED LIFE
S — Self is on the throne
† — Christ is outside the life
● — Interests are directed by self, often resulting in discord and frustration

CHRIST-DIRECTED LIFE
† — Christ is in the life and on the throne
S — Self is yielding to Christ
● — Interests are directed by Christ, resulting in harmony with God's plan

Which circle best represents your life? Which circle would you like to have represent your life?

The following explains how you can invite Jesus Christ into your life:

YOU CAN RECEIVE CHRIST RIGHT NOW BY FAITH THROUGH PRAYER

(Prayer is talking with God)

God knows your heart and is not so concerned with your words as He is with the attitude of your heart. The following is a suggested prayer:

"Lord Jesus, I want to know You personally. Thank You for dying on the cross for my sins. I open the door of my life and receive You as my Savior and Lord. Thank You for forgiving my sins and giving me eternal life. Take control of the throne of my life. Make me the kind of person You want me to be."

Does this prayer express the desire of your heart?

If it does, pray this prayer right now, and Christ will come into your life, as He promised.

How to Know That Christ Is in Your Life

Did you receive Christ into your life? According to His promise in Revelation 3:20, where is Christ right now in relation to you? Christ said that He would come into your life and be your friend so you can know Him personally. Would He mislead you? On what authority do you know that God has answered your prayer? (The trustworthiness of God Himself and His Word.)

The Bible Promises Eternal Life to All Who Receive Christ

"And the witness is this, that God has given us eternal life, and this life is in His Son. He who has the Son has the life; he who does not have the Son of God does not have the life. These things I have written to you who believe in the name of the Son of God, in order that you may know that you have eternal life" (1 John 5:11-13).

Thank God often that Christ is in your life and that He will never leave you (Hebrews 13:5). You can know on the basis of His promise that Christ lives in you and that you have eternal life, from the very moment you invite Him in. He will not deceive you.

An important reminder . . .

DO NOT DEPEND ON FEELINGS

The promise of God's Word, the Bible – not our feelings – is our authority. The Christian lives by faith (trust) in the trustworthiness of God Himself and His Word. This train diagram illustrates the relationship between fact (God and His Word), faith (our trust in God and His Word), and feeling (the result of our faith and obedience) (John 14:21).

The train will run with or without the caboose. However, it would be useless to attempt to pull the train by the caboose. In the same way, we, as Christians, do not depend on feelings or emotions, but we place our faith (trust) in the trustworthiness of God and the promises of His Word.

Fellowship in a Good Church

God's Word admonishes us not to forsake "the assembling of ourselves together" (Hebrews 10:25). Several logs burn brightly together, but put one aside on the cold hearth and the fire goes out. So it is with your relationship with other Christians. If you do not belong to a church, do not wait to be invited. Take the initiative; call the pastor of a nearby church where Christ is honored and His Word is preached. Start this week, and make plans to attend regularly.

Suggestions for Christian Growth

Spiritual growth results from trusting Jesus Christ. "The righteous man shall live by faith" (Galatians 3:11). A life of faith will enable you to trust God increasingly with every detail of your life.

* * * * *

Notes

Chapter One

1. M. John Murray, M.D., "No Evidence of Coronary Artery Disease Among Nomadic Africans," *Internal Medicine World Report,* Vol. 3, No. 1 (January 1-14, 1988), p. 6.
2. "New Perspectives on the Clinical Management of Hypertension: Calcium Channel Blockers," *Symposium Highlights* (New York: World Health Communications, 1988), p. 1.
3. W. Dallas Hall, Elijah Saunders, Neil B. Shulman, *Hypertension in Blacks: Epidemiology, Pathophysiology, and Treatment* (New York: Yearbook Medical Publishers, Inc., 1985).
4. Hall, et al, *Hypertension In Blacks.*
5. Hall, et al, *Hypertension In Blacks.*
6. Hall, et al, *Hypertension In Blacks.*
7. F. Gilbert McMahon, M.D., *Management of Essential Hypertension* (Mount Kisco, NY: Futura Publishing Company, 1984), p. 39.
8. Norman Kaplan, M.D., "Non-pharmacological Treatment of Hypertension," *American Journal of Medicine* (October 1984).
9. Hall, et al, *Hypertension In Blacks.*
10. Jay Stein, M.D., ed. *Internal Medicine* (Boston: Little, Brown and Company, 1983).
11. John L. Decker, M.D., and Harry R. Keiser, M.D., *Understanding and Managing Hypertension* (New York: Avon Books, 1987), p. 4.

Chapter Two

1. *Encyclopedia Britannica,* vol. VII, 15th edition (Chicago, 1983), p. 856.
2. Osborn Segeberg, Jr., *Living To Be 100* (New York: Charles Scribner's Sons, 1982), p. 291.
3. *Internal Medicine World Report,* vol. 3, no. 1 (Jan 1-14, 1988), p. 6.
4. John Scharffenberg, M.D., *How You Can Live Six Extra Years* (Santa Barbara, CA: Woodbridge Press Publishing Company, 1981), p. 12.
5. Dr. Michael Jacobsen, Bonnie F. Liebman, Greg Mayer, *Salt: The Brand Name Guide to Sodium Content* (New York: Workman Publishing, 1983), p. 17.
6. Spencer Rich, "Alcohol Abuse Costs Nation $117 Billion," *The Washington Post* (November 14, 1987).
7. *Healthy People: The Surgeon General's Report On Health Promotion and Disease Prevention* (Washington, D.C.: U.S. Department of Health, Education, and Welfare, 1979), p. 125.
8. "Health, Education, and Welfare official advises more caution," *DDIB Newsletter,* 4:4, 5, 11 (September 1971).
9. Jacobsen, *Salt,* p. 34.
10. *Nonpharmacologic Approaches to the Control of High Blood Pressure,* Final Report of the Subcommittee on Nonpharmacologic Therapy of the 1984 Joint National Committee on Detection, Evaluation, and Treatment of High Boood Pressure (U.S. Department of Health and Human Services, PHS, National Institutes of Health), p. 10.
11. *Bulletin of the International Society of Cardiology* (1969), 1:1-10.
12. *Dietary Goals for the United States,* prepared by the staff of the Select Committee on Nutrition and Human Needs, United States Senate, (Washington, D.C.: U.S. Government Printing Office, February 1977), p. 1.
13. *Dietary Goals for the United States,* p. 1.
14. *Dietary Goals for the United States,* p. 3.
15. F. Gilbert McMahon, M.D., *Management of Essential Hypertension: The New Low-Dose Era,* 2nd edition (Mount Kisco, NY: Futura Publishing Company, Inc., 1984), p. 1.

16. "New Perspectives on the Clinical Management of Hypertension: Calcium Channel Blockers," *Symposium Highlights* (New York: World Health Communications, 1988).
17. McMahon, *Management of Essential Hypertension*, p. 2.
18. T. R. Harrison, editor, *Harrison's Principles of Internal Medicine*, 11th edition, (New York: McGraw-Hill Book Co., 1987) p. 1024.
19. Jacobsen, *Salt*, p. 17.
20. Neil B. Shulman, M.D., Elijah Saunders, M.D., W. Dallas Hall, M.D., *High Blood Pressure* (New York: MacMillan Publishing Company, 1987), p. 1.
21. Shulman, et. al.,*High Blood Pressure*, p. 1.
22. Jacobsen, *Salt*, p. 16.
23. Timothy N. Caris, M.D., *A Clinical Guide to Hypertension* (Littleton, MA: PSG Publishing Company, Inc., 1985), pg. 4.

Chapter Three
1. Ellen G. White, *The Ministry of Healing* (Boise, ID: Pacific Press Publishing Assn., 1942), p. 128.
2. Raymond Adams, Ivan L. Bennett, Jr., William H. Resnick, George W. Thorn, M. M. Wintrabe, *Principles of Internal Medicine*, T.R. Harrison, ed., 4th ed. (New York: McGraw-Hill Book Company, Inc., 1962), p. 238.
3. Arthur G. Guyton, M.D., *Textbook of Medical Physiology*, 5th ed. (Philadelphia: W. B. Saunders Company, 1976), p. 222.
4. Guyton, *Textbook of Medical Physiology*, p. 223.
5. Guyton, *Textbook of Medical Physiology*, p. 223.
6. Guyton, *Textbook of Medical Physiology*, p. 223.
7. Guyton, *Textbook of Medical Physiology*, p. 230.
8. Timothy N. Caris, M.D., *A Chemical Guide to Hypertension* (Littleton, MA: PSG Publishing Company, Inc., 1985), p. 14.
9. Caris, *A Chemical Guide to Hypertension*, p. 14.
10. John L. Decker, M.D., and Harry R. Keiser, M.D., eds., *Understanding and Managing Hypertension*, (New York: Avon Books, 1987) p. 6.
11. Decker and Keiser, *Understanding and Managing Hypertension*, p. 68.
12. F. Gilbert McMahon, M.D., *Management of Essential Hypertension: The New Low-Dose Era*, 2nd edition (Mount Kisco, NY: Futura Publishing Company, Inc., 1984) p. 393.

Chapter Four
1. E. Cheraskin, M.D., D.M.D., and W. M. Ringsdorf, D.M.D., M.S., *Predictive Medicine* (Boise, ID: Pacific Press Publishing, 1973), p. vii.
2. *Internal Medicine News*, Kaiser Permanente Report (April 1-14, 1987), p. 58.
3. *Internal Medicine News*, Kaiser Permanente Report (April 1-14, 1987), p. 58.
4. Cheraskin, *Predictive Medicine*, pp. 3,4.
5. Cheraskin, *Predictive Medicine*, p. 34.
6. Cheraskin, *Predictive Medicine*, pp. 61-63.
7. Cheraskin, *Predictive Medicine*, pp. 61-63.
8. Cheraskin, *Predictive Medicine*, pp. 61-63.
9. E. Cheraskin, and W. M. Ringsdorf, Jr., "Predictive Medicine: I. Definition," *Alabama Journal of Medical Science* 7:4, 444-447, (October 1970).
10. J. Stamler, D. M. Berkson, M. Levinson, H. A. Lindberg, L. Majonnier, W. A. Miller, Y. Hall, and S. L. Andelman, "Coronary Artery Disease: Status of Preventive Efforts," *Arch. Envir. Health.* 13:3, 322-335, (September 1966).
11. E. Cheraskin, W. M. Ringsdorf, Jr., A. T. S. H. Setyaadmadja, R. A. Barrett, D. W. Aspray, and S. Curry, "Cancer Proneness Profile: A Study in Weight and Blood Glucose," *Geriatrics* 23:4, 134-137, April 1968.
12. E. Cheraskin, and W. M. Ringsdorf, Jr., "Diabetic Dilemma in Dentistry," *Acta Diabetologica Latina*, 8:2, 228-277, (March-April 1971).
13. *World Health Magazine* (February/March 1981), p. 3.

14. Ellen G. White, *Counsels on Diet and Foods* (Washington, D.C.: Review & Herald Publishing Association, 1938), p. 15.
15. *Dietary Goals for the United States,* United States Senate Select Committee on Nutrition and Human Needs (Washington, D.C.: U.S. Government Printing Office, 1977).
16. *Dietary Goals for the United States.*
17. "Smoking and Cancer," *Morbidity and Mortality Weekly Report,* United States Department of Health and Human Services Center for Disease Control, February 26, 1982.
18. Harold S. Diehl, *Tobacco and Your Health: The Smoking Controversy* (New York: McGraw-Hill, 1969), pp. 1-2.
19. Diehl, *Tobacco and Your Health,* pp. 1-2.
20. *Dietary Goals for the United States.*
21. R. K. Harrison, editor, *Interpreter's Dictionary of the Bible,* vol. 2 (Nashville: Abingdon Press, 1962).
22. Philip E. Sartwell, *Preventive Medicine and Public Health,* 10th ed. (New York: Appleton-Century Crofts, 1973), p. 633.

Chapter Five

1. Chinese proverb.
2. H. P. Dustan, R. E. Schneckloth, A. C. Corcoran, et al. "The effectiveness of long-term treatment of malignant hypertension," *Circulation* (1958), 18:644-651.
3. M. Harrington, P. Kincaid-Smith, and J. McMichael, "Results of treatment in malignant hypertension: a seven-year experience in 94 cases," *British Medical Journal* (1959), 2:969-980.
4. S. Bjork, R. Sannerstedt, G. Angerwal, et al, "Treatment and Prognosis in Malignant Hypertension: Clinical follow-up of 93 patients on modern medical treatment," *Acta Med. Scand.* (1960), 166:175-187.
5. H. M. Perry, Jr., H. A. Schraeder, F. J. Catanzaro, et al, "Studies on the control of hypertension. VIII: Mortality, morbidity, and remissions during twelve years of intensive therapy," *Circulation* (1966), 33:958-972.
6. F. W. Wolff, and R. D. Kindeman, "Effects of treatment on hypertension: results of a controlled study," *Journal of Chronic Disease* (1966), 19:227-240.
7. Veterans Administration Cooperative Study Group on Antihypertensive Agents, "Effects of treatment on morbidity in hypertension. II. Results in patients with diastolic blood pressure averaging 115 through 129 mm Hg," *Journal of the American Medical Association* (1967), 202:1028-1034.
8. Veterans Administration Cooperative Study Group on Antihypertensive Agents, "Effects of treatment on morbidity in hypertension. II. Results in patients with diastolic blood pressure averaging 90 through 114 mm Hg," *Journal of the American Medical Association* (1970), 213:1143-1152.
9. Lewis Walton, Jo Ellen Walton, and John Scharffenberg, M.D., *How You Can Live Six Extra Years* (Santa Barbara, CA: Woodbridge Press Publishing Company, 1971), pp. 66-68.
10. S. I. McMillen, M.D., *None of These Diseases* (Old Tappan, NJ: Spire Books, Fleming H. Revell Company, 1963), Preface.
11. *Dietary Goals for the United States*, Select Committee on Nutrition and Human Needs, United States Senate, 1977, p. 1.
12. "Smoking and Cancer," *Morbidity and Mortality Weekly Report,* (United States Department of Health and Human Services, Center for Disease Control, February 26, 1982).

Chapter Six

1. Osborn Segerberg, Jr., *Living to Be 100,* (New York: Charles Scribner's Sons, 1982) p. 35.

Step I

1. Dr. Norman Kaplan, *Internal Medicine News*, vol. 22, no. 6 (March 15, 1989), p. 25.
2. Dr. Norman Kaplan, *Internal Medicine News*, vol. 21, no. 23 (December 1-14, 1988), p. 27.
3. Dr. Norman Kaplan, *Internal Medicine News*, vol. 22, no. 6 (March 15, 1989) p. 25.
4. *USA Today* (February 10-12, 1989).
5. *USA Today* (February 10-12, 1989).
6. Dr. Brent M. Egan, quoted at a recent Internal Medicine Update at the University of Michigan.
7. Egan, Internal Medicine Update.
8. Dr. Norman Kaplan, *Internal Medicine News*, vol. 22, no. 14 (July 15-31, 1989), p. 2.
9. Kaplan, *Internal Medicine News*, (July 15-31, 1989), p. 2.
10. Kaplan, *Internal Medicine News*, (July 15-31, 1989) p. 2.

Step II

1. Dr. Mordecai P. Blaustein, Professor and Chairman, Department of Physiology, University of Maryland, quoted in "Pathophysiology of Hypertension," *Dialogues in Hypertension, Hypertension Update*, Vol. II, p. 1.
2. Dr. Michael Jacobsen, et al, *Salt: The Brand Name Guide to Sodium Content* (New York: Workman Publishing, 1983), p. 17.
3. F. Robert McMahon, M.D., *Management of Essential Hypertension*, 2nd ed., (Mount Kisco, NY: Futura Publishing Company, Inc., 1984) p. 39.
4. McMahon, *Management of Essential Hypertension*, p. 33.
5. McMahon, *Management of Essential Hypertension*, p. 19.
6. McMahon, *Management of Essential Hypertension*, p. 38.
7. McMahon, *Management of Essential Hypertension*, p. 41.
8. T. C. Beard, H. M. Cooke, et al, "Randomized controlled trial of a no-added-sodium diet for mild hypertension" (Lancet, 1982), pp. 455-458.
9. McMahon, *Management of Essential Hypertension*, p. 54.
10. Jacobsen, *Salt*, pp. 40-41.
11. F. Ericsson, B. Carlmark, K. Eliasson, et al, "Potassium in whole body and skeletal muscle in untreated primary hypertension," *International Symposium on Potassium, Blood Pressure, and Cardiovascular Disease. Excerpta Medica* (in press), 1983.
12. C. Mazzola and E. Guffanti, "Cardiovascular modification after K+ supplementation in hypertensive patients," *International Symposium on Potassium, Blood Pressure, and Cardiovascular Disease. Excerpta Medica* (in press), 1983.
13. N. Sasaki, T. Mitsuhashi, and S. Fukushi, "Effect of ingestion of large amounts of apples on blood pressure in farmers in Akita prefecture," *Igaku Seibutsugaku*, 51:103-105, 1959.
14. Jacobsen, *Salt*, p. 41.
15. Keith C. Ferdinand, M.D., "Hypertension in Blacks, Controversies, Current Concepts, and Practical Applications," *Internal Medicine for the Specialist*, vol. 10, no. 8 (Plainsboro, NJ: Med Publishing, Inc., 1989), p. 71.
16. Jacobsen, *Salt*, p. 40.

Step III

1. O. Roman, A. L. Camuzzi, E. Villalon, and C. Klenner, "Physical training program in arterial hypertension: a long term prospective follow-up," *Cardiology* (1981), 67:230-243.
2. Raymond Moore and Dorothy Moore, *Home Made Health* (Waco, TX: Word Books, 1986), pp. 134-135.
3. Westheim, Simonson, Schamann, et al, *Journal of Hypertension* (Supplement 3, 1985), pp. 5479-5481.
4. Jennings, Nelson, Dewas, Korner, et al, *Journal of Hypertension* (Supplement 6, 1986), pp. 5659-5661.

5. Somers, Conway, and Sleight, *Journal of Hypertension* (Supplement 6, 1986), pp. 5657-5658.
6. Somers, Conway, and Sleight, *Journal of Hypertension* (Supplement 6, 1986), pp. 5657-5658.
7. Westheim, Simonson, Schamann, et al, *Journal of Hypertension* (Supplement 3, 1985), pp. 5479-5481.
8. Westheim, Simonson, Schamann, et al, *Journal of Hypertension* (Supplement 3, 1985), pp. 5479-5481.
9. Jennings, Nelson, Dewar, Korner, *Journal of Hypertension.*
10. Jennings, Nelson, Dewar, Korner, *Journal of Hypertension.*
11. Charles Kuntzleman, *Diet Face* (Arbor, MI: Arbor Press, 1988).
12. *New England Journal of Medicine*, vol. 314, no. 10 (1986).
13. Mervyn Hardinge, Ph.D., M.D., M.P.H., *Philosophy of Health*, p. 14.
14. Editorial, "Black Health," *Daily Exercise*, vol. 1, no. 1 (Summer 1988), p. 7.
15. Frederich T. Zugibe, M.D., *14 Days to a Healthy Heart* (New York: Avon Books, 1986), p. 39.
16. Zugibe, *14 Days to a Healthy Heart*, p. 39.

Step IV

1. S. I. McMillen, M.D., *None of These Diseases* (Old Tappan, NJ: Fleming H. Revell Company, 1963), p. 80.
2. McMillen, *None of These Diseases*, p. 81.
3. Jay Stein, *Medicine*, p. 625.
4. *Non-Pharmacological Approaches to the Control of High Blood Pressure*, U. S. Department of Health and Human Services, Public Health Service, National Institutes of Health, 1984 Joint National Committee on Detection, Evaluation, and Treatment of High Blood Pressure, p. 14.
5. W. Dallas Hall, et al, *Hypertension in Blacks* (Chicago: Yearbook Medical Publishers, Inc., 1985), p. 171.
6. F. Robert McMahon, M. D., *Management of Essential Hypertension*, 2nd edition (Mount Kisco, NT: Futura Publihsing Company, Inc., 1984), p. 62.
7. Herbert Benson, M.D., "Relaxation Responses," *New England Journal of Medicine* (1977), quoted in *Hypertension in Blacks*, p. 171.
8. "Breathing Exercises, Group Therapy Each Found to Curb Mild Hypertension," *Internal Medicine News* (January 15-31, 1987).
9. Dr. M. J. Irvine, Psychiatric Research Department, Toronto General Hospital, *Internal Medicine News* (January 15-31, 1987).
10. Dr. Stewart Agnes, Stanford University, School of Medicine, *Internal Medicine News* (October 15-31, 1987).

Step V

1. "Yellowstone National Park," *Encyclopedia Britannica Micropedia*, 15th ed., Vol. X, 1983, p. 150.
2. "Hot Springs National Park," *Encyclopedia Britannica Micropedia*, 15th ed., Vol. V, 1983, p. 150.
3. Mervyn Hardinge, M.D., *A Philosophy of Health* (Loma Linda, CA: School of Health, Loma Linda University, 1978), pp. 39-40.
4. C. A. Mills, *Medical Climatology* (Springfield, IL: Charles C. Thomas, 1939).
5. S. Benson, "Volume Changes in Organs Induced by the Local Application of External Heat and Cold and by Diathermy," *Arch. Phys. Ther.* 15:133 (February, 1934).
6. Fred B. Moor, M.D., *Manual of Hydrotherapy and Massage* (Mountain View, CA: Pacific Press Publishing Association, 1964), p. 2.
7. D. I. Abrahamson, R. E. Mitchell, S. Turk, Y. Bell, and A. M. Zayas, "Changes in Blood Flow, Oxygen Uptake and Tissue Temperatures Produced by Topical Applications of Wet Heat," *Arch. Phys. Med & Rehab.* 42:305 (May 1961).
8. Abrahamson, et al, "Changes in Blood Flow . . . "
9. Moor, *Manual of Hydrotherapy and Massage*, p. 16.

10. E. M. Krusen, K. G. Wakim, U. M. Leden, G. M. Martin, E. C. Elkins, "Effect of Hot Packs on the Peripheral Circulation," *Arch. of Phys. Med & Rehab.* 31:145 (March 1950).
11. Moor, *Manual of Hydrotherapy and Massage*, p. 4
12. Moor, *Manual of Hydrotherapy and Massage*, p. 7.
13. "Hot Springs National Park," *Encylopedia Britannica*, p. 150.
14. Moor, *Manual of Hydrotherapy and Massage*, p. 7.

Step VI

1. *The Feminine Mistake* (Santa Monica, CA: Pyramid Films).
2. "Non-Pharmacologic Approaches to the Control of High Blood Pressure," U.S. Department of Health and Human Services, Public Health Service, National Institutes of Health, 1984 Joint National Committee on Detection, Evaluation, and Treatment of High Blood Pressure, p. 11.
3. Dr. Marc Rivo, Acting Chief of the Bureau of Cancer Control, D.C. Government, quoted in *The Washington Post* (January 25, 1987).
4. Rivo, *The Washington Post* (January 25, 1987).
5. "Normative Aging Study," *Internal Medicine News*, vol. 21, no. 4 (February 15, 1988).
6. Dr. G. C. Kabat, and Dr. Ernst L. Wynder, American Health Foundation, *Internal Medicine News*, vol. 21, no. 5 (March 1-14, 1988).
7. *Primary Care Newsletter*, a publication of The American Cancer Society, vol. 1, no. 1 (Spring 1989).
8. "World Report," *Internal Medicine World Report*, vol. 2, no. 2, (1987).
9. Dr. Dan LeGrady, *American Journal of Epidemiology* (1987), 126:803-12.
10. Dr. Walter Greensberg and Dr. David Shapiro, University of California, Los Angeles, School of Medicine, *Internal Medicine News*, vol. 20, no. 17 (September 1, 1987).
11. Dr. Lynn Rosenberg, Boston University, School of Medicine, *Internal Medicine News*, vol. 21, no. 24 (December 15, 1988).
12. Dr. Stephen Freestone, Royal Infirmary of Edinburgh, *Internal Medicine News*, vol. 20, no. 19 (September 1, 1987).

Step VII

1. W. H. Davis, *The Family Album of Favorite Poems*, p. 248.
2. "Blood Pressure Responds to Happiness, Anxiety," *Internal Medicine News*, vol. 20, no. 3 (February 1-14, 1987).
3. *Internal Medicine News*, vol. 20, no. 19 (October 1, 1987).
4. Rita Robinson, "He Who Laughs Lasts," *Vibrant Life* (September/October 1989), p. 5.
5. Robinson, "He Who Laughs Lasts," p. 5.
6. Norman Cousins, *The Anatomy of an Illness* (New York: Bantam Books, 1979), p. 27.
7. Richard Rahe, M.D., "Anxiety and Physical Illness," *The Journal of Clinical Psychiatry*, vol. 49, no. 10, supplement (October 1988), pp. 13-16.
8. Rahe, "Anxiety and Physical Illness," pp. 13-16.
9. Osborn Segerberg, *Living to Be 100* (New York: Charles Scribner's Sons, 1982), p. 7.
10. "How Can I Keep From Singing?" *Christ in Song* (Glendale, CA: Hosanna House, 1975), p. 331.
11. "Contact With Pets Appears to Reduce Heart Rate, BP," *Internal Medicine News*, vol. 20, no. 22 (November 15-30, 1987).
12. Regina Sara Ryan and John W. Travis, M.D., *Wellness Workbook* (Berkeley, CA: Ten Speed Press, 1981), p. 51.
13. "Questionnaire Helps Pick Hypertensives for Lifestyle Modification," *Internal Medicine News*, vol. 20, no. 19 (October 1-14, 1987).
14. "Questionnaire Helps Pick Hypertensives . . . ," *Internal Medicine News* (October 1-14, 1987).

Step VIII

1. *Non-Pharmacological Treatment of Hypertension,* U. S. Department of Health and Human Services, Public Health Service, National Institutes of Health, Joint National Committee on Detection, Evaluation, and Treatment of High Blood Pressure, p. 14.
2. I. L. Rause, L. J. Beilin, "Editorial Review: Vegetarian Diet and Blood Pressure," *Journal of Hypertension,* 198:2:231-240.
3. *Reader's Digest* (February 1975).
4. Julian M. Whitaker, M.D., *Reversing Heart Disease* (New York: Warner Books, 1985), pp. 60-61.
5. Whitaker, *Reversing Heart Disease,* pp. 60-61.
6. Joyce McKinnell, *The Minus Meat Cook Book* (London: George Allen & Union, Ltd., 1967), p. 13.
7. Ned Willard, "One Man's Meat," *World Health Magazine* (December 1980), p. 18.
8. Paul F. Basch, *International Health* (New York: Oxford University Press, 1978).
9. Robert L. Smith, ed., *The Best of Total Health* (Ventura, CA: Regal Books, 1982), pp. 8-9.
10. *New York Times,* Science Section (November 15, 1988).
11. *New York Times,* (November 15, 1988).
12. S. L. DeShay, M.D., "Ethical Implications of a Biblical Theology of Healing," Howard University School of Divinity, 1982, p. 97.
13. Richard W. Schwarz, *John Harvey Kellogg, M.D.* (Nashville, TN: Southern Publishing Association, 1970), p. 38.
14. Richard Schwarz, *John Harvey Kellogg, M.D.,* p. 78.

Step IX

1. Robert L. Hammond, *Almost All You Ever Wanted to Know About Alcohol* (Lansing, MI: American Businessmen's Research Foundation, 1985), p. 27.
2. Hammond, *Almost All You Ever Wanted . . . ,* p. 27.
3. Hammond, *Almost All You Ever Wanted . . . ,* p. 27.
4. International Commission for the Prevention of Alcoholism Dispatch (May 1989).
5. ICPA, U.S. Department of Health & Human Services.
6. *Internal Medicine News,* vol. 20, no. 10 (May 15-31, 1987).
7. Timothy N. Caris, M.D., *A Clinical Guide to High Blood Pressure* (Littleton, MA: PSG Publishing Company, Inc., 1984), p. 87.
8. Peter D. Arkwright, Lawrence J. Beilin, Ian L. Rause and Reobert Vandonger, "Alcohol, Personality and Predisposition to Essential Hypertension," *Journal of Hypertension* (1983), 1:365-371.
9. Arkwright, 1:365-371.
10. "Nonpharmacologic Approaches to the Control of High Blood Pressure," U. S. Department of Health and Human Services, Public Health Service, National Institutes of Health (1984), p. 10.
11. Paul B. Beeson, M.D., and Walsh McDermott, M.D., eds., *Textbook of Medicine,* 14th edition (Philadelphia: W. B. Saunders Company, 1975), p. 1055.
12. *Alcoholism Briefs* (February 1989), p. 4.
13. Hammond, *Almost All You Ever Wanted to Know . . . ,* p. 1.
14. Hammond, *Almost All You Ever Wanted to Know . . . ,* p. 23.
15. International Commission for the Prevention of Alcoholism Dispatch (May 1989), p. 3.
16. "Nonpharmacologic Approaches to the Control of High Blood Pressure", p. vii.
17. "U.S. Cancer Capital Under Fire," *Washington Post* (January 25, 1987).

Step X

1. "New Study Says Diet Can Heal Arteries," *New York Times* (November 15, 1988).
2. "Interest Growing in Monounsaturated Olive Oil as Dietary Means to Reduce LDL Cholesterol," *Cardiovascular News* (April 1987).
3. "Blood Pressure Dropped With Diet High in Monounsaturated Fats," *Internal Medicine News* (September 15-30, 1988).

4. "Blood Pressure Dropped..." *Internal Medicine News* (September 15-30, 1988).
5. "Will Olive Oil Lower Your Blood Pressure?" *Tufts University Diet and Nutrition Letter*, vol. 5, no. 7 (September 1987).
6. "Will Olive Oil Lower . . . ?" *Tufts* (September 1987).
7. *American Journal of Clinical Nutrition*, 44:635-42, 1986.
8. "Diet Rich in Animal Fat Tied to Incidence of Certain Kinds of Cancer," *Internal Medicine News*, vol. 20, no. 6 (March 15-31, 1987).
9. "Diet Rich in Animal Fat . . . *Internal Medicine News* (March 15-31, 1987).
10. "Diet Rich in Animal Fat . . . *Internal Medicine News* (March 15-31, 1987).
11. "Diet Rich in Animal Fat . . . *Internal Medicine News* (March 15-31, 1987).
12. "Diet Rich in Animal Fat . . . *Internal Medicine News* (March 15-31, 1987).
13. "Diet Rich in Animal Fat . . . *Internal Medicine News* (March 15-31, 1987); and *Cardiovascular News* (April 1987).
14. "Blood Pressure Dropped..." *Internal Medicine News* (September 15-30, 1988).

Step XI

1. J. Raymond Johnson, B. E. Pollack, H. S. Mayerson, and Henry Laurens, "The Effect of Carbon Arc Radiation on Blood Pressure and Cardiac Output," *American Journal of Physiology*, vol. 114 (Baltimore, MD: n.p., 1935), p. 594.
2. Johnson, "The Effect of Carbon Arc Radiation . . . ," p. 594.
3. Johnson, "The Effect of Carbon Arc Radiation . . . ," p. 594.
4. Johnson, "The Effect of Carbon Arc Radiation . . . ," p. 594.
5. Marvyn G. Hardinge, M.D., "The Sun: Bane and Blessing," *Ministry* (January 1989).
6. Hardinge, "The Sun: Bane and Blessing."
7. Henry Laurens, "Effects of Carbon Arc Radiation on Blood Pressure and Cardiac Output," *Archives of Physical Therapy, X-Ray, Radium*, vol. XVII, no. 1 (January 1936).
8. Laurens, "Effects of Carbon Arc Radiation . . . ."
9. *Encyclopedia Britannica*, vol. X, 15th ed., 1983, p. 247.
10. Johnson, "The Effect of Carbon Arc Radiation . . . ."
11. Fred B. Moor, et al, *Op Cit*, p. 99.

Step XII

1. Brenda Becker, ed., *Heartbeat Magazine* (n.d.), p. 28.
2. Melbourne Hovel, M.D., Ph.D., *American Journal of Public Health*, vol. 72, no. 4 (April 1982).
3. Brenda Becker, *Heartbeat*, p. 28.
4. Brenda Becker, *Heartbeat*, p. 28.
5. *Handbook of Hypertension*, p. 135.
6. Melbourne Hovel, *American Journal of Public Health* (April 1982).
7. *Current Medical Diagnosis and Treatment* (Los Altos, CA: Lange Medical Publications, 1987), p. 797.
8. *Current Medical Diagnosis and Treatment* (1987), p. 797.
9. *Current Medical Diagnosis and Treatment* (1987), p. 797.
10. *Current Medical Diagnosis and Treatment* (1987), p. 797.
11. Ray L. Walford, M.D., *Maximum Life Span* (Yew York: W. W. Norton and Company, 1983), p. 110.
12. Walford, p. 103.
13. Walford, p. 103.

Step XIII

1. Richard Cruz-Coke, M.D., et al, "Influence of Migration on Blood Pressure of Easter Islanders," *The Lancet* (March 28, 1964).
2. Y. K. Seedat, "Race, Environment, and Blood Pressure," *Journal of Hypertension* (1983), 1:7-12.
3. *Internal Medicine News*, vol. 19, no. 24 (February 1, 1987).

4. Neil R. Poulter, Kaytee Khaw, Burton E. Hopwood, Mutuma Mugambi, "Determinants of Blood Pressure Changes Due to Urbanization," *Journal of Hypertension* (1985, Suppl. 3), pp. 5375-5377.
5. Shapiro, et al, "Behavioral Methods in the Treatment of Hypertension," *Annals of Internal Medicine,* vol. 89, no. 5 (May 1977).
6. Richard Cruz-Coke, "Influence of Migration."

Step XIV
1. R. S. Paffenbarger, M. D., "Work Level," *American Journal of Epidemiology,* 105:200-213, 1977.
2. Julian Whitaker, M.D., *Reversing Heart Disease* (New York: Warner Books, 1985), p. 159-160.
3. *Journal of the American Medical Association,* vol. 224, no. 4 (April 23, 1973).
4. Jay Stein, *Medicine,* p. 625.
5. "Tie Between Diagnosis and Occupation Is Often Missed," *Internal Medicine News,* vol. 22, no. 11 (June 1-14), 1989.

Step XV
1. Engstrom and MacKenzie, *Managing Your Time* (Grand Rapids, MI: Zondervan Publishing Company, 1967), pp. 21-26.
2. Hans Selye, M.D., *The Stress of Life* (New York: McGraw-Hill Book Company, 1956).
3. Arnold A Hutschnecker, M.D., *The Will to Live,* rev. ed. (Englewood Cliffs, NJ: Prentice-Hall, 1966).
4. Homer A Rodeheaver, "I Walk With the King" (Hagerstown: Review & Herald Publishing Association, 1926).
5. Herbert Benson, M.D., "Systematic Hypertension and the Relaxation Response," *New England Journal of Medicine,* vol. 296, no. 20 (May 19, 1977) p. 1152.

Chapter Eight
1. Julian Whitaker, M.D., *Reversing Heart Disease* (New York: Warner Books, 1985), p. 84.
2. Timothy N. Caris, M.D., *A Clinical Guide to Hypertension* (Littleton, MA: PSG Publishing Company, Inc., 1985), pp. 3-4.
3. F. Gilbert McMahon, M.D., *Management of Essential Hypertension: The New Low-Dose Era,* 2nd ed. (Mount Kisco, NY: Futura Publishing Company, Inc., 1984), p. 1.
4. McMahon, *Management of Essential Hypertension,* pp. 11-12.
5. McMahon, *Management of Essential Hypertension,* pp. 11-12.
6. T. R. Harrison, editor, *Harrison's Principles of Internal Medicine,* 11th ed. (New York: McGraw-Hill Book Company, 1987), p. 1026.
7. Paul B. Beeson, M.D., and Walsh McDermott, M.D., *Textbook of Medicine,* 14th ed. (Philadelphia, PA: W. B. Saunders Company, 1975), pp. 985-986.
8. John L. Decker, M.D., and Harry R. Keiser, M.D., eds., *Understanding and Managing Hypertension* (New York: Avon Books, 1987), p. 10.
9. Decker and Keiser, *Understanding and Managing Hypertension,* p. 12.
10. Decker and Keiser, *Understanding and Managing Hypertension,* p. 6.

Chapter Nine
1. Neil B. Shulman, M.D., Elijah Saunders, M.D., W. Dallas Hall, M.D., *High Blood Pressure,* (New York: Macmillan Publishing Co., 1987) p. 68.
2. Cleaves M. Bennett, *Control Your High Blood Pressure Without Drugs (In Twelve Weeks),* (Garden City, NY: Doubleday & Co., Inc.) p. 228.
3. F. Gilbert McMahon, M.D., *Management of Essential Hypertension: The New Low-Dose Era,* 2nd edition, (Mount Kisco, NY: Futura Publishing Company, Inc., 1984) p. 75.
4. Cleaves M. Bennett, *Control Your High Blood Pressure Without Drugs (In Twelve Weeks),* p. 239.
5. McMahon, *Management of Essential Hypertension,* p. 277.

6. McMahon, *Management of Essential Hypertension,* p. 357.
7. Timothy N. Caris, M.D. *A Clinical Guide to Hypertension,* (Littleton, MA: PSG Publishing Company, Inc., 1985) p. 165.
8. Shulman, et. al., *High Blood Pressure,* p. 71.
9. R. W. Wilkins and W. E. Judson, "The Use for Rauwolfia Serpentina in Hypertensive Patients," *New England Journal of Medicine,* 1953:248:48-53.
10. R. J. Vakie, "A Clinical Trial of Rauwolfia Serpentina in Essential Hypertension," *British Heart Journal* (1949), 11:350-355.
11. Wilkins and Judson, "The Use for Rauwolfia Serpentina . . . ," pp. 48-53.
12. Wilkins and Judson, "The Use for Rauwolfia Serpentina . . . ," pp. 48-53.
13. Shulman, et al, *High Blood Pressure.*

Chapter Ten

1. Jeremiah Stamler, M.D., et. al., *The Hypertension Handbook.*
2. Letter from Paine Webber.
3. G. E. Bauer, S. N. Hunyor, and G. Stokes, "Advertising and the Treatment of Hypertension," *Handbook of Hypertension, vol. 6: Epidemicology of Hypertension,* C. J. Bulpitt, editor, Elsevier Science Publishers, B.V. 1985.
4. Neil B. Shulman, "Medication Costs Held Barrier to Blood Pressure Control," *Internal Medicine News,* vol. 20, no. 11 (June 1-14, 1987).
5. Shulman, "Medication Costs..."
6. "Black Males and Life Expectancy," *Black Enterprise* (May 1990), p. 41.
7. "Why the Inheritance Boom Is for Real," *U.S. News & World Report* (May 7, 1990), p. 33.
8. Chart—Safeway/Peoples
9. Bauer, et. al., "Advertising and the Treatment of Hypertension."
10. Bauer, et. al., "Advertising and the Treatment of Hypertension," p.507.
11. Bauer, et. al., "Advertising and the Treatment of Hypertension," p. 496.
12. Dr. Steno Julius, "Say Only 10% of Borderline Hypertensives Need Medication," *Internal Medicine News,* vol. 21, no. 14 (July 15-31, 1988).
13. From a recent Seminar for the Promotion of Hypertensive Medication.
14. Weekly Medicine Conference, Washington Adventist Hospital, 1989.
15. P. Hertzman, and B. Lindgren, (1980) Sjukdomarnas Samhallsekonomiska Kostnader 1964-75. Meddelande, 1 HE, 2, Lund.
16. Lars Wilhelmsen, *Cost-effectiveness, Handbook of Hypertension, vol. 6: Epidemicology of Hypertension, C. J. Bulpitt, Editor, Elsevier Science Publishers, B.V. 1985.*

Chapter Eleven

1. Fred Rasner, *Medicine in the Bible and the Talmud,* (New York: KTAV Publishing House, Inc., 1977) p.4.
2. S. I. McMillen, M.D., *None of These Diseases,* (Old Tappan, New Jersey: Fleming H. Revell Company, 1977), p. 13.
3. See Deuteronomy 21:20,21 (KJV).
4. Paul Tournier, *The Healing of Persons,* (New York: Harper & Row Publishers, Inc., 1965) p. 5.
5. R. K. Harrison, editor, *Interpreter's Dictionary of the Bible,* vol. 2 (Nashville: Abingdon Press, 1962).
6. John E. Williams, et. al., *Modern Physics,* (New York: Halt, Rinehart and Winston, Inc., 1968) p. 10.
7. John E. Williams, et. al., *Modern Physics,* p. 671.

Chapter Twelve

1. Dr. Robert Levy, Director, National Heart, Lung, and Blood Institute, National Institutes of Health, Bethesda, MD, testifying at the February 1977 Diet and Cardiovascular Disease Hearing.
2. T. R. Harrison, editor, *Harrison's Principles of International Medicine,* 11th edition (New York: McGraw-Hill Book Co., 1987) p. 1015.
3. Harrison, *Harrison's Principles of International Medicine,* p. 1014.

4. Asborn Segerberg, Jr., *Living to Be 100* (New York: Charles Scribner's Sons, 1982), pp. 291-92.
5. Ray L. Walford, M.D., *Maximum Life Span* (New York: W. W. Norton & Company, 1983), p. 57.
6. Steven Findlay and Joanne Silberner, *U.S. News & World Report* (November 27, 1989), pp. 82-90.
7. Robert E. Kowalski, *The 8-Week Cholesterol Cure*, rev. ed. (New York: Harper and Row Publishers, 1989), p. 8.
8. Harrison, *Harrison's Principles of International Medicine* p. 1015.
9. Harrison, *Harrison's Principles of International Medicine.*
10. Harrison, *Harrison's Principles of International Medicine* p. 1021-22.
11. David E. Hockenga, M.D., "Can Coronary Atherosclerosis Be Halted or Reversed?" *Practical Cardiology* (October 1986).
12. R. W. St. Clair, *Prag. Cardiovasc. Dis.*, 26:109, 1983.
13. R. W. Wisser, *Arter.*, 5:398, 1979.
14. N. B. Myant, *Adv. Exp. Emd. Biol.*, 168:139, 1984.
15. A. C. Arntzenius, et al, *New England Journal of Medicine*, 312:805, 1985.
16. Hockenga, "Can Coronary Atherosclerosis Be Halted or Reversed?"
17. *The New York Times* (November 15, 1988).
18. *The New York Times* (November 15, 1988).
19. *The New York Times* (November 15, 1988).
20. *The New York Times* (November 15, 1988).
21. *The New York Times* (November 15, 1988).
22. *The New York Times* (November 15, 1988).
23. Findlay and Silberner, *U.S. News & World Report*, pp. 82-90.

Chapter 13

1. Rousseau.

Chapter 14

1. E. G. White, *Ministry of Healing*, (Boise, ID: Pacific Press Publishing Association, 1942) p. 163.

Chapter 15

1. E. G. White, *Ministry of Healing* (Boise, ID: Pacific Press Publishing Association, 1942), p. 127.

Epilogue

1. Anna Letitia Barbauld, "Life," *The Family Album of Favorite Poems*, P. Edwards Ernest, ed. (New York: Grosset & Dunlop Publishers, 1959), p. 81.
2. *Bircher-Benner Nutrition Plan for High Blood Pressure Problems*, Ralph Bircher, M.D., ed., translated by Kenneth C. Taylor (New York: Pyramid Publications, 1977), p. 26.
3. Julian M. Whitaker, M.D., *Reversing Heart Disease* (New York: Warner Books, 1985), p. 90.
4. Keith Ferdinand, M.D., "Hypertension in Blacks: Controversies, Current Concepts, and Practical Applications," *Internal Medicine for the Specialist*, (Plainsboro, NJ: MED Publishing, 1989), p. 62.
5. Louisa Fletcher, "The Land of Beginning Again," *The Best Loved Poems of the American People*, Hazel Felleman, ed. (Garden City, NY: Garden City Books, 1958), p. 101.